Indian Runner Ducks

Complete Owners Guide

Published by ROC Publishing 2014

Table of Contents

Foreword

Indian Runner Ducks are often referred to as the "penguin duck" for a very good reason indeed — they stand up and they run unlike any other duck you will ever see. To watch a group of these creatures running will make you think, for just an instant, that you've stepped back in time.

In terms of pets or companions Indian Runner Ducks are often dismissed as having little to give. However, as a lover and caretaker of Indian runner ducks for 9 years I can assure you that this is far from true – irresistibly cute these comical creatures are more than capable of integrating into your daily family life. With their amazing, unique personalities they have provided hours of endless fun and fascination for us all, playing fetch with our Yorkie and driving with my daughter and I on short shopping trips - they really do have a way of bringing a certain calm and 'otherness' that is almost unexplainable.

My girls and boys range from 16 inches – 21 inches and are all well adapted for the place they occupy in their environment. These cheeky ducks love their indoor and outdoor life, busily forging and enthusiastically running around their garden, often around our house too.

Living with Indian Runner Ducks may be extremely rewarding, but experience has taught me that it shouldn't be taken lightly, the decision requires much thought and planning – runner ducks do become extremely attached to their human caregivers and it is a decision you shouldn't take lightly and is truly a lifelong commitment. However, once you make this decision to share your life with Runner Ducks, believe me, you'll never look back and have some great best friends for life.

Chapter 1 – Introduction to Indian Runner Ducks

When we think of ducks, we usually imagine stout birds, waddling around quite awkwardly. Sure, they are the epitome of grace when they are in the water but ducks are usually considered to be slow creatures when they are out of the water.

If this is your perception of a duck, you will be surprised to see the beautiful and elegant Indian runner duck. This is a duck that is upright in its posture, they don't waddle, they run! Of course, that is how they get their name and are also known as 'penguin ducks' because of their posture.

For those who are keen on having ducks in their farm or garden, the Indian Runner Duck is the perfect choice, given their interesting shape, gentle nature and their pure entertainment value.

The elegant and slim Indian Runner Duck is an extremely unique breed of duck and although there is huge debate regarding their origin, (with many enthusiasts believing they were bred for their beauty and uniqueness rather than evolving from natural selection over a period of time). One thing is for sure – top breeders and associations around the world agree that it is vital the purity of the Indian runner duck breed is protected, not only for their highly prized personalities and staggering movements – but also for their amazing laying abilities.

In the following chapters, you will learn all you need about caring for Indian Runner Ducks to ensure that they are happy, healthy companions. Of course, you may not compare them to a lap dog or a cat but they are affectionate in their own quirky way, can be easily trained and are a pure delight to have around. In many ways, the Indian Runner Duck is the perfect farm or backyard pet.

Understanding Domesticated Ducks

Before you decide to bring home an Indian Runner Duck, it is essential that you understand the basics of having a domesticated duck around you. Ducks are very unique pets and Indian Runners especially require a completely different type of caring and nurturing.

Purpose of your Indian Runner Duck

The domestication of ducks serves two main purposes:

- Duck Farming
- Pets

Duck Farming

The origins of duck farming can be traced back to over thousands of years. Most breeders believe that duck farming started in Southeast Asia. Although ducks have not gained the same popularity as chickens in Western farming, one can see a steady increase in this industry.

In terms of the type of meat and the convenience of farming, the Western world prefers to rear chickens. However, duck farming is extremely popular in countries like China where they are reared for their eggs, meat and also their down. Down, for those of you who are unfamiliar, is soft fur-like layer that you find beneath the feathers of the duck. This is used to make warm clothing in many parts of the world, promoting duck farming in those regions.

It is possible to rear ducks in cages, barn and batteries. Free range is obviously the healthiest and kindest option, especially breeds like the Indian Runner Duck. For those who are looking at making profits by rearing ducks for eggs, this is an elaborate process that requires you to pay close attention to the egg laying patterns of the female ducks. Unlike chickens, ducks are not really reliable when it comes to sitting their eggs and hatching them. In most cases, incubation is mandatory.

Ducks as pets

Many people simply love to have ducks as pets running free in their garden, farm or backyard. If you have a space large enough then believe me, they will thank you (and your life will be changed forever....)

Indian Runner Ducks also love the indoor life, so bringing them into your home is a serious option if you can cope with their cheeky demands.

Showing

Because of the ornamental value of these ducks, several breeders have worked towards making the crest and the tufts of these ducks more attractive. Even the color of the plumage has been extensively experimented with to give you the ideal ornamental duck.

It is this quality of the Indian Runner Duck that also makes it suitable for shows and competitions. If you have an Indian Runner Duck, you can enter your pet in open contests that are not restricted by memberships. Of course, if you are members of associations that specialize in duck breeding, you can enter your beloved pet in more prestigious competitions.

Indian Runner Ducks make **FANTASTIC** pets

- **They are not as messy as the other breeds**
- **They are also a lot easier to handle**
- **They love to snuggle up in warm corners of your home**

……..making them perfect outdoor or indoor pets.

Essentials of Keeping Ducks

Whether you are bringing home a duck for duck farming or to keep it as a pet, there are a few things that are absolutely mandatory:

- Ducks must have plenty of water around them. Having a duck pond is a great idea as your pets will engage in hunting for frogs and slugs.

- It is best to bring home pairs or groups of ducks. Ducks prefer to be in the company of other ducks. They feel secure and will remain active when they have the right companions.

- A coop or shelter is mandatory as ducks are always in danger of falling prey to wild beasts and even your other pets. If you must leave your ducks unsupervised, getting them a coop is a must.

- Escape is often the leading causes of death in Indian Runner Ducks that are kept as pets. They get out of the enclosure, 'run' away from their usual source of water, dry out, and die - that or running into a busy road. Since these little guys are great escape artists, and don't realize they're likely committing suicide by doing so, a secure, fenced environment is an absolute must.

History of the Indian Runner Duck

Indian Runner Duck (*Anasplatyrhynchosdomesticus*)

Runner ducks were discovered on carvings made of stone over one thousand years ago on the Indonesian islands of Java. Later found in Malaya and Lombok during the mid-nineteenth century, European explorers noted these agile and determined foragers in their accounts of their explorations. Indian Runner ducks have also appeared in a number of Dutch paintings from the early1600s.

The origin of the Indian Runner duck, however, has often been a subject of debate. While many believe that the breed must have originated in India because of its name, this is not entirely true. However, deriving from the cave paintings and other historical records, it is quite obvious that this breed originated from East Indies.

Also, Indian Runner Ducks and their eggs were salted and preserved by sailors on the ships that traded with the Dutch East Indies during the early 1600s – hence the name 'Indian' Runner Duck. Of course, the name is quite explicit. However, there is more to this breed than its roots. It has been developed and improved in several countries, giving us various colors and types of Indian Runners.

Often referred to as "penguin ducks' due to their unique stance and erect walk they were noted not only as a peculiar, flightless breed of duck but also for being prolific egg layers and it is believed the first of the eggs were sailed back to Britain on rice boats in 1835.

However, the circumstantial evidence that is available shows that these oriental ducks might have reached Europe and England well before the 19th century. There are several records of ships carrying cargos of salted 'pingouins'. This could have been the name of the Indian Runner Ducks back then. In addition to that, duck eggs were sent back in the same cargos to the Cape of Good Hope.

Paintings by Dutch masters, as early as the 1600s, suggest that the existence of a certain breed of ducks that very distinctly resembles the Indian Runner Duck. The shape and the color patterns of these ducks are strikingly similar to the modern Indian Runner Duck.

What is certain from all these findings are that the Indian Runner Duck was not bred to some breeder's fancy. They were not made to merely look exotic and pretty. This breed was developed over a long period of time in the Far East. They were bred to be hardy and agile. The most important characteristics that the breeders wanted were prolific egg laying and also a good size to make for a meaty table bird. Many breeds describe the Indian Runner as a breed with 'ample flesh' for the size of the body and fine flavor of the flesh as well.

Records made in the 19th Century suggest that Indian Runners were originally reared for their eggs. The eggs formed the main diet of the inhabitants of the region in which these birds were bred and were also available for very low costs, making them a great option for sailors who often set off on long voyages.

Indian Runner Ducks gained popularity in England and Europe in the 19th Century once they were recognized for their egg-laying abilities.

Today, the Indian Runner Duck is known for far more than just this - well known for the several color genes varieties, its charming and quirky personality and the unusual stance that makes it an absolute delight to look at and interact with.

Physical Characteristics of the Indian Runner Duck

The development of the Indian Runner Duck breed lead to the formation of several physical standards that these birds came to be known by. If you are considering showing an Indian Runner Duck then it is necessary to maintain the following standards.

Shape

The Indian Runner Duck is possibly the most recognizable duck in history due to its unusual upright pose, its striking shape and bone definition, all of which contribute to their unique status in the duck world.

When they are excited or when they are at attention, their body is almost completely upright. When these ducks are absolutely straight, you will actually be able to see a correct line from the back of their head to the tail.

However, when they are relaxed, they tend to keep their body inclined at an angle between 50-70 degrees.

Where other will ducks 'waddle', these ducks will 'run'. The reason Indian Runner Ducks are literally able to 'run' is the unusual placement of a set of very strong legs positioned right at the far rear of their bodies.

Runner ducks are a very light breed, thus contributing to their agile abilities, super speed and amazing strength. Their strong legs are easily able to carry the slender, upright bodies and their long necks, frantically foraging and generally getting up to mischief.

The total length of the duck is measured from the tip of its bill to the middle toe. A drake (male duck) usually measures between 65 and 80 cm while a hen (female duck) measures between 60 and 70 cm.

Head

The head of the Indian Runner Duck is noticeably wedge shaped, displaying an unusually straight bill with eyes that are placed high on the skull. This is not a duck you can easily mistake!

The head is normally lean and streamlined to help the duck run better. The bill has a very obvious wedge shape and fits perfectly into the flat-topped skull. The eyes of the Indian Runner Duck are particularly interesting. They are bright and alert and have a characteristic fullness. They eyes are placed so high that they sometimes seem to be above the skill line.

Neck

The neck is always in line with the body. The slender, long neck is an important feature of the Indian Runner. There is one part of the neck that is muscular and well-marked. It stands out and has a layer of hard feathers around it making it accentuate this muscular region. Usually, the proportion of the body to the neck is 2:1.

Body

The body of the Indian Runner Duck almost projects a very comic figure. It is narrow and long and maintains a characteristic cylindrical shape throughout. It is flattened only around the shoulders and sort of funnels towards the body.

Other Features

The tail is one very interesting feature of the Indian Runner Duck. When the bird is alert the tail will extend downwards towards the ground. It makes a straight line from the back, down to the ground. The wings are usually clipped when these birds are domesticated. However, the size of the wings is considerably small in comparison to the size of the body. It is very tightly packed against the sides of the birds with a crossing near the rump. The plumage is not exactly soft. It is smooth though and is tightly packed. The position of the legs, as we know, allows this bird to maintain the upright posture. The legs are medium sized and have evident thighs and shanks.

Indian Runner Ducks are generally medium sized and weigh between 1.6- 2.3 kilos for a male and between 1.4- 2.0 kilos for a female.

Defects

These physical defects are not a major concern unless you want a show duck, then the following 'defects' may spell disaster:

- A rounded or dome shaped skull
- A plump head
- Eyes placed below the top of the skull, almost centrally.
- A concave line on the surface of the culmen
- A neck that is slightly arched
- Length of the neck more than 1/3rd the total body length
- An obvious expansion in the neck giving it a 'hock bottle' shape
- Thick and short neck
- Protrusion in the shoulders that makes it prominent
- Displacement of the neck from the usually 180 degrees position giving it a hollow back appearance.
- An apparent concavity between the shoulder blades making the back look gutted
- A prominent sternum making the breast look pointed
- Very evident sternum muscles making the duck look like a pigeon
- A shallow body which appears broad, giving the bird a cricket bat like appearance.
- An obvious distortion in the trademark cylindrical shape.
- A short stern that stands evidently clear off the ground

- A long stern that grazes the ground
- Legs that have protruding and angular thighs making the carriage of the duck poor, appearing like they are placed forward, quite awkwardly.
- A tail that is turned up instead of pointing towards the ground when the bird is alert.

Other minor defects like the Roman Bill and prominent thighs that might be overlooked even in show birds.

Color Variation

Designer Ducks became a popular trend towards the twentieth century. These ducks were created only for their visual appeal. This trend had a great impact on the Indian Runner Duck. Breeders sought to improve the color variations in this breed by mixing them with several domestic breed. In fact, duck breeds like the Khaki Campbell are the result of breeding the Indian Runner Duck with other domestic varieties.

With the availability of several chromotypes and the inherent egg laying abilities of the Indian Runner Duck, both commercial and exhibition breeders took great interest in this particular breed.

The Indian Runners that were originally found in Asia were known for their beautiful plumage colors. The mutations were rather interesting. There were dusky variants, brown variants and also buff variants in this particular breed.

However, the colors that actually grabbed the attention of breeders was the exquisite fawn and white tones. These tones were natural to the Indian runners and were also found in other duck breeds like the Silver Appleyard and the Rouen Clair.

It was several years later that the pied, blue and the black varieties were introduced in the market. With the introduction of this breed came the possibility of creating a palette of colors for the Indian Runner ducks. Several stable color forms are available today, even without crossing them with regular waterfowl.

The usual color variants in the Indian Runner Duck include

- **Mallard**
- **Trout**
- **Blue Trout**
- **Apricot trout**
- **Fawn**
- **Black**
- **Chocolate**
- **Fawn and white**
- **American Fawn and White**
- **Cumberland Blue**
- **Silver**

Depending upon the breeder that you are buying your duck from, you will be able to get most or all of the colors mentioned above. Breeders are constantly in the pursuit of new colors and new varieties of these ducks. There is also ample research available to help them breed the ducks safely, after thoroughly understanding the effect of mixing various genotypes.

Personality of the Indian Runner Duck

Of all the breeds of ducks that are seen on farms and in gardens, the Indian Runner Duck is undoubtedly the most entertaining. This queer bird that looks and even walks like a penguin is highly active, foraging and running around in your garden.

As for their personality, several owners might refer to these ducks are 'comedians'. Of course, they are not your quintessential lap pet. However, these comical ducks can make excellent companions. If you spend time with them and allow them into the indoors, they will snuggle and cuddle with you. But remember, they must initiate the 'snuggle', not you.

Indian Runner Ducks are usually very calm and are very easy to handle. It is possible to train your Indian Runner Duck if you start early enough. Remember, you must always give your duck enough space to feel comfortable.

Runner ducks are usually calm and will mind their business unless you excite them for no reason. For instance, if your ducks have settled down and you suddenly switch a light on, expect them to be vocal and loud about it. They don't even like to be cornered and will panic when they are. Quite frankly, who likes to be cornered, anyway?

Vocalization

Ducks are highly communicative creatures. The Indian Runner Duck in particular loves to communicate and is quite vocal. With familiarity, these ducks will also respond to calls of their owners.

You will notice that it is usually the female that resorts to loud quacks. The male usually only creates a sound that seems like a hoarse whisper. These ducks are much less noisy than a call duck. However, they can make quite a rattle when they are excited, playful or even agitated.

Indian runners can resort to a wide range of calls including coos, grunts and whistles. In some rare cases they will also yodel. All in all, you can be sure that your Indian Runner will talk to you and communicate with you on a regular basis. So, they do make great pets and provide a very comforting companionship.

Sociability

Indian runner Ducks are quite social. They are friendly and can be tamed to be timid. However, the nature of your duck depends on several things. Usually the biggest difference comes with the gender of the birds. Males tend to be more dominating and are extremely territorial. The females, on the other hand, are quite pleasant in their nature.

Indian Runner Ducks are known to get severely attached to one person. Sometimes, they may even take a liking to your other pets. They will follow the person or pet that they are attached to. They will also be extremely possessive. If the person whom these ducks get attached to, fondle or fuss over someone else before them, they will show you who the real boss is and are known to chase and bite when they are hungry or annoyed.

All in all, Indian Ducks are extremely sociable and will only react unusually to sudden and unwanted changes in their immediate environment. Indian Runner Ducks are best when they are in groups. It is never advisable to keep single ducks at home. You can have a few males and females in the group in order to create familiarity and also to promote breeding if required.

Habitat and Distribution of Indian Runner Ducks

Although the roots of the Indian Runner Duck lie in the East Indies, this breed is scattered all over the globe. They have been domesticated for almost thousand years. They are found in almost all regions including England, Australia and America.

The Indian Runner Duck was exported by Dutch sailors to several parts in Britain. That is how they were introduced in the European areas. They were bred in America and other regions for their prolific egg laying. With an increase in the colors and variations of the Indian Runner Ducks, they also became extremely popular among exhibitors. When their commercial and exhibition values became well known, they were taken to bred in various parts of the world.

The advantage with Indian Runners is the fact that they are quite easy to maintain. All you need to ensure is that the area is fenced so that your runner ducks don't run away!

These breeds are most often found in areas with ample water, usually, around ponds. However, they are ideal for both farm breeding and also for backyard breeding. Like any other duck, the Indian Runner Duck, too, is usually found near fresh waters. They are naturally found in woodlands around lagoons, streams and ponds. They love to forage. This means that they should be in an environment where they will have access to ample wild foods, they should be able to forage for slugs and even frogs.

The Indian Runner Ducks, females in particular, require a lot of sunshine. They should also have ample dry ground to run around in. At night, they must have shelter from the wind. They should also have a comfortable roosting spot at night.

You must only consider having Indian Runners if you are able to provide a healthy environment that they can thrive in.

The following chapter will tell you what you need to do in order to prepare yourself to have an Indian runner at home.

Chapter 2: Preparing for your Indian Runner Duck

Indian runner ducks are one of the most popular duck breeds in the world. Therefore, you should easily be able to source reputable breeders who will specialize in Indian Runner Ducks.

Be completely certain about the choice that you are making in terms of the color and the purpose of the duck that you are purchasing – are they for breeding, for their amazing eggs, are you looking for a cute and cheeky pet or are you wanting to rescue a runner duck?

If you are planning on showing your duck, then you must also be certain that the duck does not have any defects that will make it an entirely worthless investment. If your duckling or duck has birth defects or has serious health issues, you will end up spending a lot more that you planned.

MAKE SURE YOU ARE AWARE of all the standards that have been set to ensure the authenticity of the breed.

As mentioned before, there are evident physical standards that you can look for in the Indian Runner Duck. However, when it comes to the actual investment, there is far more to the Indian Runner Duck than you can imagine.

What you should know before buying

The first and the most important thing when you are buying a duck is BE PREPARED.

Sure, they look cute and adorable when they are ducklings. But, they don't remain that way. If you are bringing home a duckling, be prepared to have a creature that looks and behaves entirely differently before summer strikes.

Yes, that is how fast the Indian Runner Ducks grow and that is why here is a list of things that you must know before you actually commit.

- Ducks are a long term commitment. They will usually live up to 10- 20 years. Sometimes, they may even survive longer depending upon the lineage.

- Ducks grow really fast. They are almost the size of a fully grown adult duck in just about 30 days.

- It is possible for people to acquire diseases from ducks as they tend to transmit salmonella.

- Quality duck food is essential. These foods must contain at least 15% proteins.

- They must not be given medicated food or water. This can be fatal as it causes choking and even intestinal damage in some cases.

- A duck is a rather fragile creature. This means that they can injure their neck and their wings quite easily if they are neglected. Also, since ducks are exotic pets, any ordinary vet will not suffice to give your duck the complete care it requires. You will have to look for an exotic pet vet. Be warned, these vets are extremely expensive. It is important for you to be familiar with duck care thoroughly before you make a purchase. Remember, ducks are prone to several diseases and illnesses. Not only are they difficult and expensive to cure, they may also be transmitted to humans if proper care is not taken.

- Their environment requires constant attention and care. You must make sure you keep enough clean water for them to drink every day, the bedding must be dry and the shelter must be maintained spotlessly.

- Although the Indian runner duck looks comical and is very entertaining, they are highly intelligent creatures. They are not strangers to emotions. They feel sadness and depression almost as easily and as intensely as humans. So, you must be prepared to give your ducks a lot of attention. Especially, if you plan to have them as indoor pets, you must spend a good amount of time with them. They tend to get really depressed when they are left by themselves.

- These ducks have no sphincters. To make this clearer, let me explain what a sphincter is. Sphincters are muscles that we can voluntarily control while passing bowels. So, if you think you can train your Indian Runner to 'hold it in' you are mistaken. These birds cannot be toilet trained and can therefore prove to be quite messy.

- You cannot return a duck to the wilderness. Once they have been imprinted by humans, they won't even survive a few months on their own. In many places, this act is considered inhumane and illegal.

- Indian Runners must be kept in houses or within fences. Caging them is an act of animal cruelty. Owing to their keen interest in running away, you must make sure you secure your space before you invest.

- A domesticated breed like the Indian Runner is entirely different from a wild cousin. Since they are also flightless, they must be kept away from predators and any potential danger as they do not have the option of 'flying to safety' when they are attacked.

Health Precautions

Unlike other pets that you would have at home, having poultry or waterfowl requires you to take several precautions to ensure that you do not contract any ailments from bacteria and parasites that are present on the body of the duck. Many vets actually call ducks "the Trojan horses" of germs. So if you have a pet duck or if you are breeding ducks for a business, you must be aware of the fact that they may cause serious health issues if you do not take the right measures.

Most poultry and waterfowl carry Salmonella which is a very harmful strain of bacteria. Even if you do not really come in contact with the runner ducks directly, just being in their immediate environment puts you at the risk of contracting deadly diseases.

Salmonella lives naturally in the intestines of runner ducks. Irrespective of the type of feed or the kind of care you take of your runner ducks, salmonella will be present. While Salmonella and ducks share a symbiotic relationship, humans can be severely affected. There are several ways of getting salmonella infections if you have runner ducks around you:

- The droppings and feathers of the birds carry salmonella, even when birds appear absolutely healthy.

- The cages and coops might be infected with salmonella.

- While foraging through their natural environment, ducks leave behind salmonella. This means that every part of your home where the ducks roam about is at the risk of being a potential carrier.

- The clothing and shoes of people who interact with birds, feed them, collect their eggs and even clean their living area are often breeding grounds for salmonella.

- Any contact with your mouth or the area around the mouth can lead to salmonella infections. Therefore, you must take a lot of care when you are dealing with runner ducks.

What precautions should I take?

- Wash your hands thoroughly after you have handled the birds. If you have little children at home, always supervise when they are washing their hands. You need not come in direct contact with the birds to mandatorily wash your hands. Even if your ducks are free range and you have just walked around in their living area, make sure you wash your hands before you eat. When you remove the clothes and shoes that you wore while collecting eggs or handling the birds, wash your hands.

- Make sure you thoroughly clean all the equipment that you use to take care of the birds. This includes the buckets, water hoses, rakes, feeding containers etc.

- Never allow children below the age of five to touch or handle the birds. Even the elderly or pregnant women should never come in direct contact with the ducks. These groups of people have a weaker immune system and are most susceptible to infections from Salmonella.

- Avoid allowing your runner duck to roam freely in the kitchen and the bathroom.

- If you consume duck eggs, make sure that they are thoroughly cooked before you consume them. Sometimes, salmonella passes from the intestine if the hen to the egg. The egg might be a carrier even if it looks perfectly healthy.

Signs and Symptoms of Salmonella infection

The common signs of salmonella infection are:

- Vomiting
- Diarrhea
- Persistent Fever
- Cramps in the abdomen

The symptoms in the groups of people with lower immunity are far more severe. In many cases, individuals who have been affected by salmonella must be admitted in a hospital for thorough care. They are usually recommended antibiotics to help them recover quickly.

Even if you have the slightest suspicion of a salmonella infection, make sure your see a doctor.

Where to Buy

When you are ready to make an investment in an Indian runner, you have two options that will work best for you:

- **Buying Ducklings**
- **Adopting a Duck**

Buying Ducklings

There are many pet stores and online stores where you will find Indian Runner Ducklings on sale. However, it is recommended that you buy your ducklings from a well-known breeder. The most important thing about an Indian Runner Duck is the fact that it is a purebred duck with unique features. Therefore, the lineage of your pet is extremely important, especially if you are considering exhibition as an option for your pet. On an average, the cost of the Indian Runner Duck ranges from $6- $50 or £3 to £25. When you buy from a proper breeder, you can also be sure of the parents of your ducklings. That way, you can be certain that it has no diseases or health issues.

Adopting a Duck

Very rarely, ducklings are abandoned by their mothers. In such cases, you may step in and offer to take care of the bird. Of course, there are also several birds that may be wounded or even abused. In such cases you need to be very careful and must take the following precautions before bringing your duck home:

- Check the health thoroughly. If your duck has any infection, you must ensure that it is not transmitted to humans.

- Make sure you get the right treatment for his wounds and infections. This will not only protect you and your family from contracting diseases, it will also ensure that the life span of your bird is increased.

- Has your duck suffered abuse in the past? These ducks may have issues with trusting people and other pets. Take additional care to avoid any agitation and aggression.

Choosing a healthy Indian Runner Duck

If you are aware of the standards necessary to purchase a healthy Indian Runner duck, you can be certain that the breeder will not give you a duck that is not worth its cost. There are five important things that you must look for while buying a duck or a duckling:

- The body must be lean and refined. You must be able to see the unique cylindrical shape that is characteristic of an adult runner duck.

- The top of the head must be smooth. If it is rough, it is the sign of possible health issues and also improper breeding.

- The eyes must be wide and active and must be paced centrally on the head.

- The depth from the top of the skull to the bottom of the jaw must be very small.

- The plumage should be smooth and free from knots and bumps.

A list of defects has been mentioned in Chapter 1. That will also be extremely handy when you are choosing the ducks that you want to take home with you.

Duck or Duckling?

For new duck owners, this can be a very difficult question. Should you bring home an adult duck? Or should you experience the joy of actually raising a duckling till it is an adult? The answer is quite simple. It entirely depends upon what your real intention of bringing home a duck is.

For those who already have ducks at home, bringing an adult into the group is a safer bet than bringing home a duckling. A group of ducks is less likely to adopt a duckling with the chances of getting along with an adult bird a lot higher.

Another reason for bringing home an adult duck is adoption. If you want to give shelter to a wounded or abandoned duck, it is a great and noble ideal. However, with these ducks you must take necessary precautions and quarantine measures.

Benefits of Ducklings

- You can actually take care of your Indian Runner from a young chick.

- The temperament of the duckling will be as per your bringing up. You can train them to be highly sociable and gentle when you rear them from the baby years.

- It is easier to make a duckling personable. You can teach those tricks easily when they are ducklings.

- You can be sure of the health of your duckling. Since it has been with you all along, you can be certain that it is free from parasites and infections.

- If you are looking at raising ducks in a farm alongside other animals, it is advisable to bring home ducklings. They are able to get along with other animals easily when they grow up in the same environment.

Benefits of Ducks

- If you want to your duck to be an addition to an already existing group of pet ducks, an adult duck is a better choice.

- Those who are looking at a lucrative business will benefit by including healthy adult ducks instead of ducklings. There is no need to wait for the duckling to grow into an adult. You can also save on the investments required to raise a duckling.

- You can provide a safer environment to a duck that has been abandoned or orphaned.

- Exhibitors benefit by bringing home well-bred show ducks instead of ducklings. The cost of raising is reduced in this case.

Irrespective of whether you are bringing home an adult duck or a baby duck, you must be highly cautious about the health of the bird. In several cases, even a healthy looking duck might carry salmonella in its feathers and feet.

Taking ample quarantine measure is important when you are considering a pet duck.

Quarantine Measures

The biggest threat with ducks is the possibility of infections and if you are considering an indoor pet, then especially, you must take additional quarantine measures to ensure the safety of your family.

How Salmonella is transmitted

Ducks usually carry salmonella on their bodies, within their plumes and on their feet. They will also release salmonella in their droppings. Therefore, people around the ducks are constantly in the danger of coming in touch with Salmonella.

These germs are not restricted to the body and feces of the bird. Everything that your duck comes in contact with is infected. This includes the cage, the soil, the plants and even the clothing of people who handle the birds. So when someone unknowingly comes in contact with any of these elements in a duck's environment, they are likely to be infected. The biggest problem arises when the hand or object that is infected with Salmonella reaches the area around the mouth.

Children are at maximum risk of infection as their immune system is not entirely developed. In addition to that, children have the tendency to put their fingers in their mouths. It is possible to avoid infections by taking simple measures.

The simplest thing to do is washing your hands every time you handle the duck or come in contact with their immediate environment. This sounds quite doable for both adults and infants. However, there is one section of your family that is still in danger. Yes, I am talking about other ducks and pets that you may have.

Sometimes, a new bird may have infections that will prove fatal to ducks and other fowl present in your farm or garden. The only way to overcome this is by taking adequate measures to quarantine.

Quarantining requires you to keep the new bird away from the rest of the birds for at least 2 to 3 weeks. During this period, your new bird will require a separate coop or house to ensure that he does not mingle with the birds. Many duck owners neglect quarantining to avoid the expense of an additional coop. However, it is worth the investment considering that the entire existing flock is in danger of infection.

While your duck is in quarantine, you must make sure that you give it highly nutritious foods. With Indian Runner Ducks, giving Vitamin tonics are also recommended to help take care of injuries, if any.

In case you have two separate flocks of birds, make sure you disinfect yourself while dealing with either group. This means that you must wash your hands thoroughly, change your clothes and even use separate equipment for these two groups. This will ensure that neither of them comes down with an infection that the other might have and actually be immune to!

Imprinting

Among the various types and breeds of domestic fowl, the Indian Runner Duck is believed to be highly compatible with humans. In general, ducks are the second most suitable companions for human beings. In first place are geese that are known to get highly attached to their human friends. This relationship is built because of a unique ability possessed by these birds. This is known as imprinting.

The concept of imprinting is rather interesting. The process of this phenomenon is yet to be explained. Nobody knows what exactly happens in the brain of the duck when an imprint is formed. The first and the strongest type of imprint is the filial imprint.

Filial Imprinting is a certain belief pattern in these ducks. As soon as these birds hatch, the first being that they see is recognized as their mother. If you remember watching baby ducks in the wild or even in films, they follow their mothers around and are very keen on obtaining the attention of their mother. Now, it is not necessary that the mother has to be a duck. If you are the first being that a duck sees upon hatching, it is automatically imprinted in its brain that you are mom. Of course, these ducklings are unable to recognize the face or voice of their imprinted parent. However, they will follow you around and expect you to be their mom.

Now, some of you may think that imprinting might be true in case of dogs and cats or other pets, too. After all, they are equally attached to their owners. However, there is one very distinct difference between other animals and birds like ducks and geese.

No matter how attached a dog or cat is to you, it will always recognize itself as a dog or cat respectively. However, when a duckling forms an imprint, it believes that it is the same creature as its parent. So if the imprint formed is that of a human, a duck will believe that he is human.

Even if there are other ducks present around it, the ducking never sees them as parents. It is possible for the duck to understand that he is not a human but is a duck, when he is around others of his own species. However, the filial imprint is only of the being he saw first. The other ducks are only imprinted as his siblings. He will learn and play with his siblings. However, the beauty of this breed is that he will love his 'mom' the most.

If you are planning to hatch eggs, remember that your responsibility does not end with successfully bringing a duckling into this world. If the baby sees you first after hatching, you are in for a long term commitment. You will have to play the role of the duckling's mother. Therefore, if you are planning on incubating and hatching a duck egg to bring home a duckling, there are a few things that you must ask yourself.

Do You Have the Time to Be Mom?

Once the duckling believes that you are mom, you are in this relationship for the long run. This is actually a full time job. You will have to sleep next to the duckling, play with him outdoors, eat with him, ensure that he is warm, console him when he is crying and even learn to speak the language of the ducking. The only possible break you will get is a short time away from the duckling when he is in the hands of a trained and experienced duck sitter.

Will you be patient enough?

There is no way you can litter train your Indian runner duck. They are not capable of controlling their poop. They will mess up your home. Despite being the parent, you cannot even think of disciplining these babies. Even a gentle flick or smack can injure their delicate bills and bones. You might be tempted to use duck diapers but be assured that your babies will absolutely resent it.

What are the resources you have?

Although your duckling may think it is a human, the truth is that he will grow up to be a fully grown duck whose needs are just the same as any other duck. You must be able to give him a shelter that is free from predators. It is your job to ensure that he eats well and gets the required healthcare. There are also several additional expenses that you will be responsible for.

If you wish to parent a duckling, you must be completely committed. It is also your responsibility to ensure that your duckling interacts with his own species for breeding purposes in the future. Remember - if you have pets at home, you are responsible for their safety at all times.

The concept of filial imprinting is quite adorable. However, the responsibility of the parent is far more than taking care of the bird. There is another important concept known as sexual imprinting that you must also be aware of to ensure that your duck grows up and picks the right mate for himself. Although this seems quite natural in the animal world, the way a duck thinks will bewilder you.

Sexual Imprinting

Sexual imprinting is a very important phenomenon in reproduction and breeding. It is through sexual imprinting that a certain species recognizes the attractive features in an opposite gender of the same species. It is with this understanding of attractive features that the bird picks the right mate when it is mature.

With ducks, sexual imprinting works quite differently. The roots of sexual imprinting lie in filial imprinting. Now, if the duck recognizes another duck as its mom, there lies no issue. However, in case the filial imprint is that of a human, it is a task for the human to help this duckling grow up to recognize his own species as desirable to mate with.

If you are planning to hatch an egg, you must make sure that there are several other ducks that this duckling can grow around. In case this does not happen, the duckling will view the features of the human as attractive. So, there are high chances that he will court other people or even the parent instead of other ducks. He might find his entire species altogether unattractive. Now, if this happens and your purpose of having an Indian Runner Duck is its prolific egg laying quality, think of the consequences.

Therefore, you must be very knowledgeable about the phenomenon of imprinting. You must also realize that a duck may not be safe in the environment of the human mother. Think of the several things in your immediate environment that can harm your birds. Bobby pins and buttons, for instance seem mundane to us. However, for curious creatures like the Runner Duck, they could become that fatal snack. So when you take charge of a duck egg, remember your responsibility.

Types of Housing for Indian Runner Ducks

Ducks are usually meant to be free range pets. This means that they should be allowed to walk and run freely, however IT IS ESSESNTIAL that the space must be guarded or enclosed.

- Predators are always on the prowl. Since these ducks are flightless, they make very easy targets. They cannot escape by flying away from danger like other ducks in the wild.

- Runner Ducks have this name for a reason. Yes, they are capable of running pretty fast but are also capable of running away. If the space that they are kept in is not enclosed, they might wander away and be seriously injured.

- Free range pets are most often killed by traffic. If your farm or home is close to a busy freeway, you must be additionally cautious when you bring home a duck.

- Ducks require a warm shelter at night to remain healthy. Ducks, in particular, love a calm and secluded place to roost at night. They may feel uncomfortable and even threatened if that does not happen.

Fencing the area around your home is a great idea when you have a duck. However, you will need to house your ducks in the right place so that they are able to rest well and stay healthy. There are several options available. The Indian Runner Ducks in particular are quite easy to house as they can be trained and handled easily.

Duckling Housing

The first stage of housing a duckling involves the creation of a "brooder". Also known as a hot house, the brooder is a warm housing option that is extremely essential for baby ducks. The temperature of the housing must be kept high as ducklings require the warmth that their mothers provide them with.

You have several options with duckling brooders. They differ in their shape. You can get simple boxes that look like batteries and even ones with canopies that resemble space ships. The heat source could be electricity or even gas. In case you want to purchase brooders that are readily available, you must be prepared to shell out a lot of money.

However, preparing a brooder at home is also quite simple. All you need to do is find a regular duck house and place a heated lamp at about 90-94 degrees to keep the ducklings warm. This temperature must be lowered by about 5 degrees each week. When the ducklings are about 8 weeks old, they will develop feathers that will keep them warm. So, you can lower the temperature to about 50 degrees.

It is possible to gauge if the ducklings are comfortable or not. If they are simply lying around and are generally quite comfortable, it means that the temperature is right. However, if the temperature is low, they tend to huddle together. If it is too high, you will see them coming to the edge of the house where it is a lot cooler.

Another thing you must consider is the fact that ducklings grow really fast. Within a month, the duckling grows to the size of an adult. In the first two weeks, each ducking will only require about 0.75 square feet each. In the fourth week, you must give them at least 1.75 square feet. By the time they are six weeks old, each duck will require 2.75 square feet to himself.

Sometimes, a simple rubber tote or tub will work well if the number of ducklings you have is not too many. No matter what housing choices you make for your ducklings, make sure that it is easily maneuverable. You must also have good bedding inside. Ducklings also need guards to be set around the housing to ensure that there are no drafts at night. This will also ensure that the ducklings do not get out.

Duck Pens

Once your ducklings are the size of an adult duck, you may shift them to a pen. Of course, you will need a pen even when you adopt an adult duck. There are some general principles that you must maintain when you design a duck pen. You need not make it too lavish or elaborate. However, certain parameters should be maintained.

You have two options when it comes to housing ducks:

- **Intensive housing:** This means that for a particular season, your ducks are kept indoors.

- **Semi - Intensive housing**: The ducks are allowed to go outdoors in the mornings but are locked in their pens at night.

There are some things you must maintain in a duck pen, mandatorily

- The pen must be kept dry and clean at all times. It must be well ventilated. At the same time you must ensure that it has been sufficiently rain proofed.

- Every bird requires **at least** 0.2 sq meters of space to spread their wings and stay comfortable.

- There are chances of egg breakage and moisture inside the pen. To absorb this, you need to cover the floor with litter to a height of at least 7 cms.

- Usually, wood shavings are preferred. However, you may choose any other material that is soft and absorbent.

- When you choose a spot to build the pen, make sure that the area is sloping gently. If it is too hilly, you will not be able to build a neat pen. On the other hand, a flat surface poses drainage issues. Depending on where you live, there are local councils that will be able to give you the right advice when it comes to choosing the site to build the duck pen.

- Ideally, the pen should face north-east.

- The Indian runner duck stands upright, so you must ensure that the roof is placed at a decent height.

- Shade is absolutely necessary for all ducks as they are affected by excessive sunlight.

- When you are planning to build a duck pen, take time to make the layout and the ground design. If you are having ducklings and ducks in the same pen, you must clearly assign different areas for them. Make sure that there is no entry from one area to the other.

If you have breeding stock, the flooring is especially important. The floor must have a combination of litter and slated wired areas. With this arrangement, wet litter is not an issue. Make sure you place all the feeders and the water on the slated area. The ducks will use only the litter area to mate and lay eggs. Having a pen with only slates can result in leg injury and damage, especially in breeds like the Indian Runner Duck who like to really move around in their pens.

You may even create nests to encourage your ducks to lay eggs there. This will keep the eggs safe. The eggs are less prone to damage and will also be safe from sunlight and moisture. Each nest should be able to house only one duck at a time.

Ensure that the pens are free from drafts and locked securely at night to make sure that your ducks do not wander away.

Estimated Size of the Housing

Runner Ducks are one of the easiest breeds to accommodate. If you are planning to fence your house, you will need to keep the height at about 2.5 feet. Remember that the Indian Runner Duck is not the best flyer. The only reason for you to raise the fence and protect it with welded mesh is to keep predators and visitors outside your enclosure.

The size of the pen or the housing can never be too large, irrespective of whether your ducks are breeding or growing. The only parameter that determines the size of the housing is the number of birds you have. The thumb rule here is that you must never have more than 5 birds per sq. meter. Ducks like to have ample space around them to spread their wings, flap around and even 'stretch' in a manner. So, as the owner, this is your responsibility. The distance from the floor of the housing to the roof should be at least 2m. This will allow your Indian runners to stand upright and walk around if they want to.

Sometimes, smaller pens and housing might work just fine. However, if you see that the ducks are huddled together because of the lack of space, you must consider shifting. Of course, your ducks will have access to water for swimming. If the space is too small and crowded, it will become very muddy and dirty easily. This results in poor health and conditioning of your birds.

Once you have the right house for your birds, the challenge is to create the right environment for them to thrive healthily. You must make sure that you never compromise on the natural instincts of your Indian Runner Duck, even if he is domesticated.

Creating the Right Environment for the Indian Runner

Whether you are breeding or simply maintaining ducks in your farm or backyard, you must ensure that you create the right environment for them to feel secure and comfortable.

Swimming

Ducks are able to waterproof their plumage by secreting special oils from glands beneath their skin. This waterproofing not only helps them when they are in water, it is also extremely essential in maintaining the body temperature of the ducks. This means that the waterproofing of the plumes helps the ducks keep themselves cool in summers and also warm in winters. Waterproofing only occurs when the ducks swim regularly. They need to be able to bathe and immerse their entire bodies in clean water to maintain the waterproofing. You can either have brooks or even simple kiddie pools at either ends of the housing that you have made for your ducks. You must ensure that the birds have easy access to this clean water that they will utilize for swimming.

Ideally, your Indian Runner Duck must be given access to clean swimming water when he is approximately 10 weeks old. Even in this case, you must monitor them constantly until you are certain that they are able to get into the water and get out of the water by themselves.

Grass

In the wilderness, ducks are usually found near ponds and brooks that have long grass growing around them. This serves two purposes. First, the ducks are able to hide between the long blades of grass to protect themselves from predators. Second, the area between the grass provides the ideal location for foraging. This is where the duck's favorite snacks are available easily.

Likewise, even when they are domesticated or bred, ducks maintain the same attachment to grass. It is recommended that you grow grass around the the ponds that you have created for your ducks. Allow the blades to grow as long as possible. Ideally, the grass should grow taller than the Indian Runners. This will help them hide and forage just as they would in the wild.

Shades and Trees

Landscaping is an important part of owning ducks. In order to give your ducks the perfect free raging experience, you must make sure that they feel as close to nature as possible.

One thing that ducks strive for is shade. They are easily harmed by excessive sun exposure. So, having trees and bushes will provide them with the shade that they need. If you do not have room for trees in your backyard, you can even plant bushes that grow tall and thick. You will see your Indian Runners resting in their shade during the hot summer months.

Another advantage of having plenty of trees and bushes is that they will attract bugs and insects. These bugs make great food for your ducks. Foraging for bugs and snacking on them also gives your Runners something to do. When you are choosing plants, trees or even shrubs to landscape the area where you keep your ducks, you must be very careful. Some varieties can be extremely toxic for ducks. So, before you landscape you yard, do your research and understand what trees and shrubs work best with ducks.

Bedding

The best option for bedding, especially for ducklings is **rye straw**.

Remember, the bedding that you choose must provide ample cushioning and must also turn into a comfortable nest if you do not have a separate nest altogether. There are several other materials that make comfortable and warm bedding - some common choices are peanut hulls, crushed corncobs, wood shavings and even sawdust. You must make sure that the shavings are not from treated wood or from cedar trees.

The bedding material that you choose must be mold resistant as ducks will bring in moisture every time they come back after a swim.

Straw is considered a very poor bedding option, especially for ducklings. Within a few minutes of hatching, ducklings will start to forge. Anything that looks worm-like will be eaten. So, ducks and ducklings usually choke on straw. If you are, however, insistent on using straw, make sure that you choose a variety that is larger. Straw must be replaced as soon as it becomes even slightly moist.

Another important factor to remember whole choosing bedding for your ducks is the footing. If you use slippery material like newspapers, you are likely to damage the legs of the ducks. They develop a condition called 'sprawled legs' when they are forced in an environment where they do not have ample footing.

You can try different materials until you find one that your ducks like the best. All you need to ensure is that the bedding is soft, warm and completely mold resistant.

Making a Pond

For those who are planning to have ducks in their backyard, a duck pond would be a beautiful addition to the landscape. In addition to being a great place for your ducks to go for a swim and just hang out with their group, the duck pond also acts like a great aesthetic piece in your garden or backyard.

Materials you will need

Setting up the perfect pond is quite the struggle. It involves a lot of labor and can be slightly expensive if you want it to last longer. Quite frankly, for the amount of effort that you would put into engineering a duck pond, you might as well make that investment.

For the basic structure, polythene landfill liner works best. It is durable and is resistant to the roots of trees and plants. You may also choose butyl but it is not half as robust as polythene. The edges of the pond must be secured with underlay made from felt before you actually lower it in to the ground. To make the pond appear natural, burying it in gravel or even riddled soil works well. It is also useful in protecting the pond from damage caused by UV rays.

How big should the pond be?

If your pond is too shallow or too small there is a risk of temperature fluctuations and easy soiling due to the little volume of water. This causes rapid growth of algae and weed that are damaging to the health of your runner duck. In a large pond, there is no need to pump in algicide either.

Ideally, a duck pond should be at least 12 inches wide and 24 inches deep. Of course, this changes if the number of ducks is increased.

Plants in the Pond

Plants are a must in a pond that is being designed for ducks. They make the perfect spaces for the ducks to forage around and look for food. They also give the ducks a sense of security because, instinctively, ducks love to hide between water plants.

Oxygenating plants are a must for a duck pond. They will not allow algae to thrive in the water. Algae only flourish in anaerobic conditions, i.e. lack of oxygen; these plants add oxygen to the water making it impossible for algae to grow.

It is never a good idea to have plants like lotus and water lily which have floating leaves. These plants are unable to withstand the bashing around that ducks love to do. It is therefore best to plant saplings that are marginal - they will border the pond and will not have to encounter the nipping and splashing of the ducks.

Some of the best suited plants are marsh marigold, shuttlecock fern, mares tail and pickerel weed. Some varieties of marginal plants are not exactly robust. However, they will be able to survive with the ducks. The advantage of most of these marginal plants is that they will self-seed. So once they are fully grown, you need not really worry about rotating the plants or even planting new saplings.

You must always take great care while purchasing plants for your pond. If you buy weak plants, the dabbling of your ducks will only leave a big mess around the pond. The ideal plants are those that have fibrous stems and roots. You can simply plant these saplings in the soil or gravel around the pond and just allow them to grow thereafter.

Why ducks love ponds

There are several waterfowl experts who believe that swimming water is not really a necessity for runner ducks. Of course, there are several flocks where the older birds will merely dip their beaks in to the water once in a while. However, the truth is that if there is good, clean water available, your runners will love it. The younger birds and the birds that are about to breed are especially benefitted.

Remember that the slugs and the greens available at the pond will provide the best source of minerals for the younger ducks.

When you introduce a flock to the pond, especially if they are ducklings, make sure that they are initially supervised throughout their time in the water. The water must also be replaced on a regular basis as still water will soil easily. If it is left dirty, it becomes the ideal breeding ground for mosquitoes and other undesirable pests.

Safety measures

You must take some precautions and safety measure before allowing the ducks to access the pond:

- **Keep Other Wildlife away:** A pond that is out in the open may also be accessed by other wildlife. If you have seen the presence of harmless animals and birds around the pond, you need not worry. However, the presence of predators means that you must keep the possible entry points closed. Ensure that invaders are unable to enter your home in the first place.

- **Make the access easy:** If the pond is hard to get in and out of, your duck might suffer serious leg injuries. Make sure that you define the access points of the pond with gentle slopes. The ducks will be able to slide in and then waddle out when they want to.

- **Select the plants carefully:** Although there are several plants that are robust enough to survive the dabbling and the foraging of these ducks, they may not be the ideal additions to your duck pond. For instance, a common pond marginal plant, the Parrot's Tail, tends to grow quite long.

This plant might get entangled with the feet or body of the duck making it difficult for it to swim. Ducks are delicate creature and may also suffer from sprains and fractures in an attempt to free themselves from the tangles of such plants.

- **Separate the groups of ducks:** If you have ducks and ducklings in your backyard, it is a good idea to keep them from entering the pond at the same time. There have been several instances where adult drakes have held ducklings underwater and drowned them. The reason for this type of behavior is unknown. However, just keeping the ducks and ducklings away from each other is a safer option.

- **Provide Shade:** It is a common belief among duck owners that the presence of water is good enough to keep the ducks comfortable and cool. However, ducks are easily prone to sunburns. Since they might choose to spend a good amount of time in the pond, providing them with ample shade is a great idea. You can build a pond under the shade of a tree if possible. If that is not an option, artificial structures like sheets and roofs can be put up to protect the birds.

If a pond is not a possibility, even kiddie pools work really well with ducks. A pond, however, adds to the charm and appeal of having waterfowl in your backyard.

Duck Proofing your Garden

If you choose to keep ducks in your garden or backyard, duck proofing is a must. Since Indian Runners love to forage, the landscape of your garden might take a beating if you do not duck proof it sufficiently.

Ducks love to trample leaves and anything green. Although they might feed on certain leaves, in most cases, they will pull out the leaves and simply trample them. They will play with these leaves and just toss them all over your garden. If you have shrubs or plants that are less than 2 feet in height, it is a good idea to protect them with chicken wire or any other type of mesh. Once your plant or shrub grows beyond this height, you can be certain that at least the upper leaves will be spared.

Another thing that ducks love to do is sink their bills deep into the mud to look for food. If the soil is moist, it is even more attractive to these birds. So, when you water your bushes, do not be surprised if your duck pals are eager to dig small holes in the ground and dabble around in the mud. This can cause serious damage to the roots of your shrubs. The best thing to do is to ring the base of these bushes with either rocks or pavers. They will also add aesthetic value to your garden.

You may also include certain varieties of plants that your Indian Runners will stay away from. It is a known fact that ducks do not mess with shrubs belonging to the fir or evergreen families. You can plant shrubs like hawthorn, rose, juniper and even dwarf pines and be sure that your duck will stay away from it. These bushes also act as the perfect barrier against the wind and sun to protect your precious beauties.

Ducks and Other Pets

The Indian Runner Duck is a rather pleasant creature to have around. If you have other pets at home, you must make sure that in the first few months of the ducks' arrival, the interactions between your pets and the new entrants is always supervised.

You must make observations of the behavior of the ducks around your pets and vice versa. If you feel like there is any obvious tension or dislike between the animals, do not force them to be in the same space. This can be dangerous to both creatures. Remember, that Indian Runners are also highly territorial and can become aggressive when they are threatened.

Runners when kept in pairs or groups will seldom bother the other pets in your home. However, there are several instances of great friendships between runners and other pets. If they have grown up together, they should be able to bond with each other happily.

Indian Runner Ducks and Neighbors

If you plan to have Indian Runners in your backyard, you might want to be a little sensitive in relation to your neighbors. Although Indian Runner Ducks are one of the quietist species any ducks can be noisy, especially females. As we mentioned in the earlier chapters, it is only the females that make loud quacking noises.

There are ways you can minimize the noise experienced.
- First, having thick landscaping around your garden will act as a great insulation against the sound.
- Having Indian Runners in groups will reduce the noise to a large extent. Usually, females become noisy only when they are calling out their   mates.

It is a good idea to check with your local Environmental Health Department to check if your backyard is a suitable place for the ducks. If it is an inhospitable environment, expect your ducks to become noisy. You might also want to send your neighbors a circular informing them about the ducks that you might have in your yard – preparing them for an odd quack here and there.

Transporting Ducks

There are several reasons why you might have to transport your ducks. If you are shifting your home, you must ensure that you take your ducks safely with you. You might also be sending one or more ducks to another farm for breeding and mating. Even if you are only planning to move the ducks to a better and larger pen, you might have to consider various transportation options.

Transportation Options

Your Personal Vehicle

When you re transporting your runner ducks in your own vehicle, please remember that they are extremely fragile creatures. Ducklings are, especially, prone to strangulation and broken bones when they are being transported.

It is a good idea to choose proper carriers to transport your ducks. Make sure that the size is just right to prevent them from falling and hurting themselves. The bedding should be soft and thick to provide ample cushioning. You must also ensure that food and water is available to the ducks. If you are transporting adult ducks, you might want to carry them in separate carriages. If you are transporting multiple birds, make sure that they are able to see their companions so that they feel secure. While transporting ducklings, you must also provide them with a proper heat source to keep them warm.

Shipping

You may also use the postal services to transport your ducks. If you are considering shipping your duck in overnight carriages, it is important for you to obtain a health certificate from a licensed veterinarian. This rule is applicable in most states. The certificate must be obtained at least 10 days prior to shipping

The best option is the bio- safe carrier that is used to transport birds. These carriers come with a lining that is water resistant. They also have air holes to ensure oxygen supple to the bird. A substance known as gro-gel plus may be used to keep your ducks hydrated during the flight. Ideally, you will require about 2 packets per duck for an overnight flight. You can place the gel in plastic cups secured to the corners of the carriers so that the ducks have access to it throughout the journey.

It is advisable to take the package yourself to the airport that the ducks will fly out of. Your local post office will be able to give you that information.

Make sure that the flight is non-stop. Ducks cannot make it more than one non-stop flight from one city to another. If you must make a stop, ensure that the second half of the journey is covered by road or rail.

Make sure that your carrier screams out that there are live birds in it. Although there are signs on the packages usually, you must ensure that you highlight this fact. This is because any live animal is treated differently from other cargo, they are transported in areas that are safe and comfortable.

It is a good idea to line the box with warm bedding. You must also make sure that the material you use gives the duck proper foothold to prevent injuries due to skidding.

Shipping ducks in the beginning of the week is ideal as the staff remains the same. If you ship them any time after Thursday, there is a higher possibility of mix ups. Shipping or air travel should be the last option when you are transporting your ducks. If you can avoid it, make sure you do to avoid unnecessarily traumatizing of the birds.

Estimated Costs

The cost of shipping ducks, like any other shipment, depends entirely on the size of the package. Usually, a package containing less than 35 ducklings is considered a small shipment. All in all, you will spend about $50/ £30 for the shipping itself. In addition to that you will pay $50/ £30 for the box and the supplies necessary to ensure a safe trip for your birds.

Chapter 3: Indian Runner Duck Care

Indian Runner Ducks make perfect pets. They are pleasant natured and usually prefer to stick around both the humans and the ducks that they know best! They are extremely active creatures that love to run and dabble in open spaces - also highly sociable, making them perfect companions.

Handling an Indian Runner Duck

Of all the breeds of ducks used by exhibitors, the Indian Runner Duck is most preferred because of the ease with which it can be handled. They are usually very calm and will not depict any unfriendly behavior. As for human companionship, once the ducks get accustomed to it, they are VERY social and communicative. Several owners of Indian Runners vouch for the fact that their ducks love to snuggle and follow them around. However the duck must trust you completely in order to feel completely comfortable and secure.

Gaining the Trust of Indian Runner Ducks

You know that your duck trusts you completely only when they come to you on their own (not only when you offer them treats).

It is in the nature of ducks to be slightly fearing and untrusting of other species. This is because they are a species that lie at the bottom of the food chain. Therefore, they have the instinctive urge to protect themselves and only stick to their own kind.

Usually, runners will try frantically to stay away from human touch - this is natural for them. Unlike other pets, they do not instinctively like to be fondled or petted. Even when they are in groups, they will rarely touch each other intentionally - only when they are mating or fighting, so it is quite natural for them to run away at first.

The only way you can handle ducks is by studying their body language. If the ducks seem agitated and afraid, whatever you are doing is making them react that way. On the other hand, if your ducks are relaxed and calm, continue doing whatever you are doing. Make sure you read their reactions and respond accordingly. You must always try to maintain an environment where your ducks will be calm and happy.

If you offer them treats and interact with them on a regular basis, they will come to you and communicate with you. They will try to nibble your clothes and belt and even your shoes. However, if you reach out to them, they might just jump away from you.

For those who raise ducks since they were ducklings, this is not an issue at all. They will be quite familiar and comfortable with you when they grow up watching you. You know that your duck trusts you when he is able to sleep peacefully around you. Sometimes, they will even sleep on your lap quite comfortably.

Catching the Ducks

Once you have established trust, you must also learn how to catch a runner duck. The idea of catching them is not to snuggle or pet them, they instinctively dislike that. So, when you are catching your duck, it is usually to nurse wounds, clip their wings etc. You must always insist on catching your duck **only** when it is for its own good. If you tend to fondle them or catch them too much, they will associate that feeling of discomfort with you and will respond with little or no enthusiasm.

The first step towards catching a duck is to ensure that you do not startle them. Never approach them from around the corners quietly. Instead talk to your bird so that it knows you are around.

If you must catch them, lead them to a small corner, 90 degrees or less - free from any obstacles. Ducks will not move or run very fast in small corners.

If you simply leap into the catching bit without establishing trust, your duck will treat you as a predator and will flap around quite hard and will even try to leap away from you. In fact, it is easiest to catch them by their body when they leap, if you are alert enough.

You must ensure that you never catch a duck by its legs, you might cause severe damage. You must always catch hold of a duck by his neck or his body. Once you have caught your duck, remember to keep the wings in your grasp, firmly.

In case you miss, you have to allow them to settle down before you make your next attempt. When the ducks do not view you as a predator, they are a lot calmer.

Catching ducks can be a matter of great patience. Especially, with breeds like the Indian Runner Duck that actually runs pretty fast, you need to be extremely agile and alert at all times.

Flying and Wing Clipping

The process of clipping a bird's wing is usually adopted to ensure that the birds' ability to fly is reduced. However, in case of Indian Runners, this practice seems quite redundant as they are originally flightless birds. They usually tend to huddle along in groups and just forage in the open space. So, why would you want to clip their wings?

Well, the only reason most breeders clip the wings of a Runner Duck is to reduce the number of eggs laid. A runner duck with clipped wings will only lay about 25-40 eggs in the summer months. This makes it possible for the owners and breeders to keep a track of the eggs and take care of them accordingly.

Daily Care and Cleaning

The most important part of the daily care routine with Indian Runner Ducks is the cleaning. These birds require clean water and a clean enclosure to remain healthy. Feeding is important, no doubt. However, for ducks, having access to water is more important than having access to food.

You must make sure that you change the water in the water every day. This will not only ensure that the pen remains clean, it will also ensure that the plumes remain healthy. It is a good idea to keep the water at a considerable distance from the bedding to avoid soiling. If you have a make-shift duck pond, you must also clear this water out on a regular basis.

The biggest issue you will find with your Indian Runners is that they are rather messy creatures. They will poop around the clock and basically poop all over the place. You must be prepared for this when you have a pet duck, making sure that the coop of the duck is cleaned at least once a week.

Watch out for moisture in the litter and on the floor of the coop. If the coop is not kept clean, ducks develop a particular condition known as Bumblefoot. This is a bacterial infection that affects the padding on the feet of the duck. This condition makes it difficult for the runner to stand. Since they rely so much on walking and running around, leaving Bumblefoot untreated can even lead to death.

Moisture is the enemy in a coop. If you notice egg breakage or wetness in the litter, change it entirely. For this purpose, you must ensure that the opening of the coop is large enough to fit a rake through it. That way, you will be able to get the litter out quite easily.

Cleaning a duck pen or coop is tedious as they are messy creatures. If they are allowed be free range during the day, the amount of poop in the pen is reduced, making it easier for you to clean up the mess.

Feeding your Indian Runner Duck

When you take the responsibility of keeping ducks in your backyard or in your farm, you must ensure that they get ample nutrition to stay healthy. In case of Indian runners, several owners make the mistake of assuming that they will be able to survive solely on bread crumbs. This is not true. In order to breed and stay healthy, Runner Ducks require several nutrients. The main nutrients that they require include protein, calcium and phosphorous.

With breeds like the Indian Runners, their habit of foraging ensures that they are not entirely dependent on their owners for food. However, you must give them the right kinds of food to keep them and their eggs in best shape. If your duck is malnourished, you will notice a distinct decrease in the activity levels. Of course, there are several nutritional sources that ducks rely upon

Natural Foraging

The Indian Runner Duck was bred keeping the foraging nature intact. The posture of the duck is also helpful in allowing it to reach out to bugs and insects that other ducks cannot reach out to. If you own an Indian Runner Duck, you must make sure that you encourage this foraging nature as it forms the essence of their being. It helps them find the right food and also gives them a good amount of exercise.

It is a good idea to hold back duck feed on a regular basis so that your Indian Runners will rely upon foraging more. You can watch them glide in between plants, dabble the soil and pick their favorite natural treats. Usually, Indian Runner Ducks will go after slugs and toads as they form their favorite foods in the wild. On the up side, this is a great way to naturally keep your garden free from pests and insects. If you have trees with berries and fruits, the Indian Runner will gobble them up too, reducing the number of flies and bees. So, encouraging the habit of natural foraging is not only goof for your Runner Duck, it also works very well to maintain your garden or backyard in good shape.

Food Dispensers

The biggest challenge with ducks is to monitor their feed and to makes sure that they eat regularly. If you are not able to do this hands on, you can use a food dispenser.

The most basic type of food dispenser consists of a plastic dome like structure that has a roof to keep the food dry. It has a small feeder around it where the ducks can eat. The beauty of this dispenser is that it keeps refilling the feeder as the ducks finish eating. So, all you need to do is to fill the dispenser regularly and be care free.

Another interesting type of food dispenser is the tread plate feeder. With this type of feeder, a small metal tread plate provides access to the food. Every time a duck steps on this feeder, it will open the lid to the container which stores the bird feed.

Besides making your life easier, food dispensers serve several other purposes. Now, birds have very tiny digestive tracts. That's why they poop so often. Undoubtedly, they also remain hungry all the time and constantly require food. With a food dispenser you can ensure that your precious pets have access to food all the time.

A common problem that most duck owners face is finding poop in the food very often. Using a food dispenser puts an end to this rather difficult problem. Also, you will not have to deal with upturned bowls of food. This reduces wastage and ensures that the food is stored in hygienic conditions.

Automatic Pet Feeders

An automatic pet feeder is only useful when you have smaller flocks of ducks. These feeders are ideal to feed one or two pets each time. So if you have between 2 to 4 ducks, this type of feeder might work well for you.

Automatic pet feeders have been designed for people who are unable to stay at home all day to ensure that their pets are being fed on time. It is possible to program close to 10 meals each day for your Indian Runner Duck. You can set the program to dispense an exact amount of bird feed each time. You also have the option of setting different portions each time.

As mentioned earlier, Indian Runner Ducks are not really dependent on their owners for their food. They can easily forage for their food. However, In the case you have to keep your runner ducks indoors, for instance, if your duck has undergone any surgery or is under treatment, he may not be able to forage so this type of feeder works best.

Food Options for Ducks

If you own a duck, the first question that you must ask yourself is what you feed them. Many pet owners make the blunder of feeding their ducks bread crumbs. If you are concerned about the nutrition of your ducks, you must make sure that the food is appropriate for their age as well as the time of the year.

- **Natural Foods:** Usually, ducks will forage for their food. Their natural diet includes worms, insects and slugs. They also feed on grass and duck weed. When you allow your duck to obtain natural foods, you will see that the plumage is glossy and the beak has a distinct orange color.

- **Ducklings and Growers**: When you have a flock of ducklings that have just hatched, refrain from feeding them 'chick crumbs' that are available in the market. It is a good idea to provide them with duck ration that is free from preservatives and additives. You can use this starter duck ration for about 2 weeks after the eggs have hatched. After this, they must be given duck grower pellets that are not too high in their protein content. Only when the ducks have become the size of an adult that you will give them 100% grower size pellets.

- **Wheat:** Wheat is a great source of nutrition for ducks that are approximately 5 weeks old. You must give the ducks a portion of grit along with the wheat. Like most birds, ducks are unable to chew their food. So they usually consume their foods with tiny rocks and pellets that help make it more digestible for your Runner Duck. When your ducks are about 10 weeks old, you can put them on a diet which consists of 50% dry pellets and 50% wheat.

Medicated Feed

Medicated feed is usually given to birds that are prone to diseases and parasites - usually Turkeys and Chickens. However, with the understanding of common waterfowl disease, medicated feed has been extended to all breeds of ducks as well.

The most common diseases with ducks include colibacillosis , salmonellosis and fowl cholera. Colibacillosis is caused by the infection of the digestive tract and the air sacs.

Similarly, salmonellosis and fowl cholera is also caused by bacterial infections. These diseases cause a lot of weakness in the ducks and can, in many cases, result in the death of the duck. It is important to manage and control these diseases by providing the ducks with the right kind of food.

The use of medicated feed has been quite useful in several cases. However, you must also ensure that you maintain high standards of hygiene and sanitation for 100% disease prevention.

Supplements for Ducks

Unlike other farm fowl, water fowl have special nutritional requirements. For instance, ducks require a high protein diet to be healthy. At the same time, the balance in these nutrients also needs to be maintained - if the duck has excess proteins in its diet, you will notice that the feathers will start bending upwards.

Besides proteins, calcium and phosphorous also form an important part of the diet. The quality of the egg depends entirely upon the calcium consumed by the ducks. In case they are laying eggs with very thin shells, it is an indication that they are not getting enough calcium and phosphorous.

Another important nutrient required for Indian Runner Ducks is Niacin. This vitamin is essential is the correct development of the duck's legs. If you notice that your duck is not finding enough strength in its legs or is unable to walk properly, it could be a sign of Niacin deficiency.

To address these deficiencies, you can use supplements that are readily available in the market. Usually, these supplements are available in the form of tablets in all pet stores.

When you are buying supplements for your duck, make sure you consult your veterinarian. Only when they are prescribed should you include supplements in their diet as an overdose of nutrients may have adverse effects – please be extremely cautious.

Water

You must ensure that ducks are never fed without water. Many duck owners have a misconception that ducks may drink too much water and actually die. Hence they keep the water away from the ducks while feeding them.

This practice is never recommended as ducks require water more than they require food. Especially when you are feeding the ducks dry pellets, you must make sure that you provide water alongside. When ducks eat dry pellets or crumbs and fail to have an adequate amount of water, the feed begins to swell inside the duck. The risk of choking is also high when ducks are given dry food without water.

Nutritional Concerns for Laying Ducks

When your ducks are breeding and ready to lay eggs, the kind of nutrition that they require is entirely different. The food that they eat needs to be nutritious enough to ensure that the eggs are healthy.

For this, you must give them something called layers pellets. These have excess calcium and phosphorous. Usually, the best time to feed the duck layering pellets is at the end of the day. You must make sure that you get special layers pellets designed for ducks – many owners will simply feed their ducks layers pellets meant for Hens. These pellets contain too much calcium and also have additional substances like egg yolk colors.

To make the meal wholesome for the duck that is laying, you can mix these pellets with an equal portion of wheat.

You should be able to notice when your Runner duck is ready to lay eggs as the abdomen looks much fuller than usual. It is best to start providing layer pellets from the months of February as the eggs are most likely to be laid in the summer months.

The quality of the food that you provide to the ducks should be noted very carefully. Remember, a certain brand of pellet that is more expensive than the others available in the market will contain a higher concentration of vitamins A, D and E.

Avoid purchasing maintenance pellets.

For your ducks to breed and for embryos to be as healthy as possible then the correct diet is essential. If your duck is able to obtain free range food safely, this a great option when they are ready to lay eggs.

Seasonal Care

The requirements of your Indian Runner Duck change according to the season. You must be prepared to make necessary changes in the feeding, bedding and even shelter of your ducks to make sure that they are able to get through a particular season comfortably.

Although Ducks do come with some natural thermoregulation, thanks to the waterproofing of their plumage there are still several factors to be aware of.

Summer Care for ducks

During the summer months, you must be aware that the ducks will start laying eggs. So the first thing that you must take care of is the bedding of the duck or the nest. If you are able to provide a nest or bedding that is additionally cushiony, you can prevent damage to the eggs. In addition to that, you must also increase the litter on the floor of the coop.

The food that you give your duck will change in the summer months. For the ducks that are about to lay eggs, you must make sure you mix in layers pellets instead of regular duck feed pellets.

The shelter does not require any additional insulation in the summer months. However, you must be very careful and monitor sun exposure, making sure that they have ample shade available – being able to protect themselves from the blistering heat of the sun. There have been several instances when ducks have had sunstrokes because they did not get enough shade. You must also keep plenty of clean water around so that the ducks can cool themselves off when required.

Winter Care for Ducks

Indian Runner Ducks need special care during the colder months. Remember that domestic birds react to cold conditions just like the wild ducks. The difference lies in the fact that the wild birds are able to migrate to warmer places. On the other hand, the domesticated Runner Ducks will be dependent on you to provide the right environment.

The food essentially remains the same. Wheat, which is ideal for all seasons, forms the main constituent of the diet. If the weather is extremely cold, you can also opt for maize which provides the ducks with the required amount of calories to keep themselves warm.

Ducks must also have constant access to food. You can increase the feeding portions in the summer months as the ducks will require this to thrive and remain healthy in the colder months.

The shelter must be additionally insulated to make sure that the ducks stay warm. This means that the litter inside the shelter must be increased. You can also line the walls of the coop with some insulating material - the trick is to ensure ample ventilation while keeping the duck house warm.

Fighting and Separation Considerations

Runner Ducks are not naturally violent creatures. In fact, they tend to be very wary and cautious all the time. Females, especially, are extremely pleasant. However, you must never overrule the fact that they are descendants of the wild and will, hence, have some basic instincts even when they have been completely domesticated.

Runner ducks will fight and be aggressive only in some conditions. Usually, drakes are extremely territorial and do not appreciate any invasion from other species of birds. In addition, if your group of runners has several males and only a few females, the drakes will fight to find a mate. If you want your runners to keep calm then its best that you have equal numbers of males and females.

Runner Ducks are startled quite easily. They will fight back when taken by surprise. Remember, we spoke about imprinting? They are also very possessive about the imprinted parent. If they see that parent getting too close to some other bird or animal on the farm or even another human, your Runner Duck might attack.

The common signs of aggression in Runner Ducks are

- **Nipping with their bills**
- **Violent Flapping of the wings**
- **Using their strong legs to attack**
- **Loud calls**

Keeping Chickens and Runner Ducks

In many farms, Runner Ducks and Chickens are bred together. However, separation is a good idea, although there are several breeders who will suggest otherwise. While most of us might assume that the larger birds, the Runners, might harm the Chickens, it is quite contrary. Chickens are the ones with sharper beaks and are more prone to attacking and causing damage.

If you insist on keeping them in the same enclosure, make sure that they are in a large space. So, if they ever get into a fight, they will have space to move away from each other. Usually, with ample supply of food and water, the Hens and Ducks will mind their own business and will seldom get in each other's way.

Housing is a primary concern with both Ducks and Hens. Unlike hens, Ducks do not always settle down after sunset. They will take some time to roost. Also, during the breeding season, cockerels and drakes might become argumentative if they do not have enough space for themselves. So - make sure they have separate housing.

The feeders for the Ducks and Hens must be placed in separate areas - simply because the food that you give your hens is quite different from the food that the Indian Runners require. Waterers must, most definitely, be separate. Hens only drink from the waterers and get on with their business. On the other hand, Ducks need to take a dip occasionally and will make a mess of the waterer - so, the water source for the Ducks and Hens must be placed at a considerable distance from each other.

If you see signs of violence then you might want to separate their enclosure. You can even restrict the entry from one area to another using wiring and fences. Whether you want to permanently separate the two or only keep them away for particular seasons, you have necessary fencing options.

Types of Fencing

Temporary Fencing

Temporary fencing serves two purposes. It can be used to separate various farm animals and can also be used to direct them into their enclosures. The primary function of a temporary or portable fence is to mark boundaries and actually control your animal groups.

The most common type of temporary fence is the chain link fence. You can get long rolls of chain links that are arranged in a zigzag pattern. The heavy base allows you to place them where you need. Another simple type of temporary fencing is the mesh fence. It is similar to the chain link fence but is more secure as the base is heavier.

If you need to keep out larger farm animals like dogs or sheep, you can use a picket fence. They have vertically arranged wires that have a very strong base to keep these animals away from your poultry.

Chicken wires or poultry fences are the most common type of temporary fences used to keep ducks and chickens separate. These fences are ready to install and can be adjusted as per your needs. They do not require any tools for installation and work perfectly well on all terrains.

Permanent Fencing

Permanent fences do not serve the purpose of separating different farm animals. They are used to mark the boundary of your garden to prevent animals from getting out or getting in to your property. For instance, if you have a freeway near your home, a permanent fence will keep your Indian runner ducks from getting away from your garden or farm. They also keep predators at bay.

Needless to say, these structures, once installed must not be removed. They must also be able to keep small animals and birds from getting in and out. In addition, they must also be strong enough to hold on for several years.

The most common type of permanent fencing used to keep your Indian Runners Safe is the wooden or bamboo fencing. Panels of wood and bamboo are installed around the perimeter of your space. You must make sure that there are no gaps in between panels. Concrete fences are also used. They are sturdier and are also great at keeping predators away.

Electric fences are not my favorite option. Many blogs and websites suggest them as an effective way to keep predators away. However, there are chances that your own pets will get electrocuted and I personally find it a cruel option whether you are thinking of keeping predators or pets in their boundaries.

Predators

The biggest problem with having water fowl in your garden is the danger of predators. It is heartbreaking when you realize that one of your beauties has been taken away or killed by a predatory animal.

The difficult part is that ducks are usually extremely vulnerable when they are domesticated. So, they become easy prey for animals like coyotes, foxes, bobcats and raccoons. With animals like the coyote, you can even expect attacks in broad daylight. So you must take several preventive measures to ensure that your Indian runners are safe. Some methods you can use are:

- Allow your ducks out in the open. This is required for them to survive. However, if you have noticed attacks during the day, make sure you have someone to supervise the birds.

- Get rid of possible hiding spots for predators. Coyotes, especially, love hiding in thick bushes before attacking the ducks.

- Getting a dog will help if your predator problem comes from bobcats. They are effective against other animals, too. However, bob cats can be kept at bay only with dogs as no fence or enclosure will stop them.

- Direct your ducks into enclosures every night. They are difficult to pen. However, you can lure them with treats and certain sounds to make sure that they get into their enclosures at nights.

- Use fences as the primary defense against predators.

- Do not leave garbage out in the open. Usually, predators like raccoons are first attracted by the smell of the garbage. If you can keep your space clean, you can avoid such animals.

If you think that predators are a serious problem, you may also contact your Environment Protection Council. They will be able to give you more definite methods to keep predators away. If the problem still persists, keeping the ducks in spacious pens is the best option. You can still create the right environment for your ducks so that they continue to forage and have a good time.

Training the Indian Runner Duck

Indian Runner Ducks are among the favorite exhibition breeds across the globe. These birds are extremely easy to handle and can be trained just like other pets to perform simple tricks. As a result, the Indian Runner Ducks are very personable and can be quite entertaining as pets.

It is possible to train your Indian runner duck to follow simple commands. Of course, they will not "sit" or "stay" like your doggie pals. You can train them to respond to certain sights and sounds. For instance, using treats and sounding a rattle when you do so will train them to come to you when they hear the rattle. This trick works very well when you have to lead your duck into enclosures, through hoops, etc. They can also be trained to follow a certain stick or even your hand movements using this technique.

Walking your Indian Runner Ducks

The best thing about an Indian Runner Duck is their stance. Since they are able to walk upright like penguins, you can actually take them for walks. This might seem unconventional for a duck, but remember that they need their exercise.

Amongst all the different duck breeds that exist, Indian runners require the maximum amount of walking or running. This helps them maintain their lean bodies and will also give their legs enough strength. One way to make sure that they have to run or walk is to keep their feed about 50m away from their pens.

You can even walk your runner duck using a leash. You can buy a special halter leash from pet stores that are designed to go around the body of the duck rather than its neck. You will be surprised to see their enthusiasm when it comes to going on walks with their owners.

Should You Keep a Runner Duck Indoors?

This is a topic that has been often debated. Many owners dream of having house ducks that they can pet and cuddle. However, ducks are not the best indoor pets. The Indian Runner Duck, especially, is an instinctive forager and will poke through all the stuff in your home. They are also extremely messy. You must be ready to have a really smelly home if you want to keep a duck indoors. If you have children at home, you must definitely get your runner duck a comfortable space outdoors.

Sometimes, however, if the duck is ill or injured, you may have to keep it in your home for safety. In such cases, it is recommended that you use a diaper for your duck and give him a specific corner of your home to sleep and roost in.

Toys for Indian Runner Ducks

Giving your Indian runner some mental stimulation is also necessary. They can be entertained using toys. Usually, bright toys that you might use for pets like parrots will work well with your Runner ducks. Make sure that the toys you give your duck do not have tiny parts that may be swallowed accidentally.

The best toys for ducks are the squeaky toys and rattles. The noise made by these toys is rather amusing according to ducks. If you really want to bring the comedian in your duck out in the open, leave him with a mirror. He will be bewildered and excited all at the same time. You will see him walk around the mirror, nip at it and sometime simply stand and watch. Runner ducks make great playmates as they are easily excitable. These smart ducks can also be trained to play with specific toys like ladders and blocks.

Learning the Language of Ducks

If you think of ducks as nothing more than mere waterfowl, you might be forced to think again. Ducks are excellent pets to have as they are highly intelligent and extremely communicative. Of course, it does take a little effort to understand the behavior of ducks and to be able to speak their language effectively.

Communication among Indian Runner Ducks is a combination of specific sounds with their body language. Research shows that these ducks may also have regional accents or dialects just like us humans! So, it is quite easy to tell how your duck is feeling if you can just learn the language of ducks.

Vocalization

The first method of communication that ducks use is vocalization. They have different calls to signify different moods. The greeting call of a duck is usually very even toned and spaced. They will probably repeat their call three to four times to greet you.

You can know for sure when your duck is arguing with you or disagreeing with you as he will make a very specific incitement call. With males, their regular hoarse whisper is combined with a soft growl when they want to express their displeasure. When the females are agitated, by an intruder or even by drakes, they make a very loud threatening sound which is often referred to as a chuckle. This sound is very aggressive, loud and insistent. Even males might display this type of call when they are distressed.

Muttering is observed often in baby ducks that are following their "mommy". This could be you or the real mother duck. They will mutter and whisper to each other almost as if they are afraid that you might hear something.

The Body Language

Ducks are quite the attention seekers.

They love to have their owners and the other ducks in their group around them, communicating with them. Usually when a duck is happy to see you, he will respond by bobbing his head. The head bob is a straight, up and down motion of the head. This is a common display even when ducks are inviting their mates.

The feathers are also used to communicating. If your duck wants your attention, he will ruffle his wings and his tails insistently. Of course, you must not mistake a heavy flap of the wing as a call for attention. This means that your duck is either scared or afraid. When he displays this sign, make sure that you stop whatever you are doing.

It is fun to communicate with ducks when you are aware of what they mean. This is one of the most essential parts of being a duck owner. Being able to pick messages from their body language will help you take better care of them and give them everything that they require.

Chapter 4: Health and First Aid

When you have pets at home, one of the most important things is to be aware of the different health problems that your pet might face. Having the knowledge will help you get your pet the right kind of help at the right time. Usually Indian Runner Ducks live up to 12 years of age. However, with good health care and nutrition, Runner ducks are known to live up to the age of 20 or 22. In some pens, the oldest ducks are nearing 20.

So right from the time the egg hatches till the time it becomes an adult, the health of your duck must be monitored very closely. Being waterfowl, they are susceptible to several infections, some of which may also be fatal. This chapter discusses the common health problems faced by Indian runner ducks, the symptoms, signs and also the treatment required. To begin with, let us understand how you can tell if your Indian Runner Duck is healthy or not.

How to tell if your Runner Duck is Healthy?

The good thing about ducks is that they have very unique characteristics and behavior patterns. Any deviation from normalcy is a sign that your duck is either unwell, or is stressed for various reasons. There are some common symptoms that you must look out for if you suspect that your duck has fallen sick:

- Reduced levels of activity
- Not socializing. A sick duck will keep to itself and will occupy a lonely corner in the pen
- Loss of appetite
- The volume of activity is reduced
- Sudden deviation from normal activity
- Sticky poop that is found on the vent of the coop
- Eyes that are dull or half closed
- Change in the color of the poop or diarrhea
- Sleeping for long hours
- Constant Sneezing

- Puffed up feathers
- Feathers those are ragged and not preened properly.
- Sudden Weight Loss
- Swelling in the joints
- Breathing with the mouth open

Indian Runner Ducks are fabulous creatures in several ways. One very interesting display of group behavior is assisting other birds when they are unwell or injured. You can tell that a duck is unwell even by observing the behavior of other ducks around him.

For instance, if your duck has a broken wing, you will see that other ducks will gently hold up the upper feathers to provide assistance. They will also nudge and flock around unwell ducks in a caring and affectionate manner. However, you must be aware of one important thing. The above mentioned signs can be observed only if you are very vigilant. Usually, ducks are great at hiding their illnesses. Therefore, many owners are unable to tell if their ducks are unwell until it is too late.

NEVER neglect even the slightest deviation in your bird's behavior.

Common Health Problems in Indian Runner Ducks

Bill Problems

The bills of ducks are not mere defense organs, they are very important in indicating the health of the bird. Any abnormality or deformation in the bill indicates that the bird may have several underlying health issues that require immediate attention.

Signs

There are some common and obvious problems that owners might notice with the bills of their pets:

- Rotting or discolored beaks
- Cracks in the beak
- Dry beaks that are peeling
- Bruised beaks with visible brown coloration at the bruises
- Overgrown or stunted upper or lower beak

Causes

- Malnutrition, usually a deficiency in Biotin and calcium
- Possible Liver Damage
- Exposure to toxins and chemicals
- Infection and Injuries
- Applying too much pressure while hand feeding ducklings

Treatment

- Providing dietary supplements in case of malnutrition
- Removal of ticks and parasites
- Biopsy to check for secondary ailments
- Trimming of the beak

Feather and Skin Disorders

Waterfowl are susceptible to several infections of their skin because of their constant contact with water. The feathers and the wings might show some sure shot signs of an infection. There are specific symptoms that you can watch out for in such cases.

Symptoms

- Angel Wings where the feathers are turned upwards
- Constant Scratching and preening
- Bald patches in the plumes
- Wet Feathers
- Cysts and Abscesses on the skin

- Soreness and redness of the skin
- Cysts
- Slipped wings that have feathers growing outwards

Causes

- Too much protein intake, especially in case of slipped wings and angel wings
- Ecto parasites
- Ticks and Mites
- Reduced secretion of waterproofing oils by glands present in the skin. This might be due to ruptured glands or malfunctioning glands
- Cysts and abscesses are usually caused by blocked glands
- Poor living and breeding conditions
- Infections and Injuries

Treatment

- Reduced protein intake
- Providing a balanced meal with recommended pellets and wheat
- Recommended powders or medication to treat parasites, ticks and mites
- Medicated feed to resolve issues pertaining to glands
- Maintaining a healthy and sanitary environment for the birds

Respiratory Problems in Runner Ducks

If you observe your runner duck breathing with the mouth open, there are chances that he is suffering from respiratory ailments. Other common signs of respiratory problems are sounds like wheezing or whistling when the duck is breathing.

It is important to take care of respiratory problems at the earliest as they might be fatal to the duck. Ducks are also unable to function properly and carry out regular activities like foraging and running if they are unable to breathe properly. When ducks become inactive, they also become severely stressed, leading to secondary problems like behavior changes.

One important thing that you must remember when you notice that your duck has respiratory problems is that you must consult your vet before taking any action. This is because problems related to the lungs of birds can be quite complex. Remember that the lungs of birds are modified or adapted to aid flying. As a result, the treatment of respiratory problems should be left to the specialists.

Chronic Respiratory Problems

One chronic respiratory problem that is common to Indian Runner Ducks is called Alpergliosis. It is also known as brooder pneumonia or mycotic pneumonia. The symptoms of this disease are as follows:

- Labored breathing
- Hunching of the spine to aid breathing
- Whistling or wheezing noises while breathing.

Causes

Apergillosis is usually predominant in birds during the monsoon season. This is because the bedding might develop molds due to the moisture. Sometimes, poor sanitary conditions may also lead to Aspergillosis.

Treatment

- Use of fungicides
- Better management of the pen
- Storage of food in dry and cool conditions
- Use of bedding material that is resistant to molds.

Air Sac Infections

The air sacs in ducks play a very important role. Besides helping them breathe normally, air sacs are also necessary to help the birds stay afloat in water. However, these air sacs are susceptible to infections, causing chronic respiratory problems.

Symptoms

- Constant bobbing of the tail
- Labored breathing
- Salivating excessively
- Breathing with the mouth open
- Clicking and Whistling noises while breathing

Causes

Air sac infections are usually caused by parasitic mites. It may also be due to bacterial infections.

Treatment

- Anti-parasitic injections
- Oral Medication
- Reduced handling and fondling of the birds

Lameness in Indian Runner Ducks

A common problem that is found in ducks, especially Indian runner ducks is lameness. They might have difficulty in walking and sometimes, just standing up. Since runner ducks are highly dependent on their limbs for locomotion, you must ensure that you take proper care to treat lameness or other problems with the legs.

Causes

- Sprained, Broken or injured joints
- Arthritis
- Cuts in the feet
- Damage to the muscles
- Pinched Nerves
- Hip Dislocation
- Splinters in the feet
- Bacterial Infections. A common bacterial infection in ducks is called bumblefoot. This leads to abscesses on the feet that make it difficult for the bird to walk properly.
- Inflammation of the tendons
- Damage to the Kidney
- Aging

Treatment

- Examine the legs and feet for cuts and splinters
- Check for abscesses at the bottom of the foot
- Provide the right diet, especially for growers
- Calcium and vitamin supplements
- Corrective dressing and casts in case of injuries

Note: Cover of all the wires and mesh in the coop where the legs might get caught and be injured.

Digestive Problems

One of most important things to keep in mind is providing your ducks with ample water whenever you feed them. If they are unable to swallow the food or digest it properly, they will develop digestive issues.

Most of the digestive problems in birds are related to their crop. The crop is that part of the duck where the food goes immediately after feeding. You will notice a slight bulge in this region when your duck has just eaten. If the bulge does not disappear overnight, it is a problem. There are two conditions that you must look out for in Indian Runner Ducks.

Sour Crop

Symptoms

- Swollen Mucus Membranes
- Appearance of an apple lodged in the neck
- Lesions around the neck and mouth

Causes

Sour Crop is usually caused by yeast infections in the crop of the bird. This condition is dangerous as it may damage the esophagus or even strangulate the bird, leading to death.

Treatment

- Withhold food for one day
- Provide clean and fresh drinking water only
- Massage the crop
- Drop olive oil into the crop to help it reduce in size

Sour Crop must not persist for more than 3 days. If it does, it is recommended that you consult your vet.

Blocked Crop

This condition is also known as impacted crop. As the name suggests, this condition occurs when the crop of the duck gets blocked.

Symptoms

- Difficulty in swallowing
- Crop that is hard to touch
- Reduced Appetite
- Foul Smell from the Beak

Cause

- Consumption of foods that are too fibrous or tough
- Consumption of long strands of straw
- Lack of water

Treatment

- Provide your duck with ample drinking water.
- If the condition persists, your vet may surgically remove the blockage in the crop.

Common Eye Problems in Ducks

When you have ducks in flocks, you must be wary of any disease that is contagious. Normally, amongst ducks, eye problems are contagious and may affect several birds at one given time.

Usually, eye problems are the symptom of some other underlying medical condition that requires attention. So, if your duck has shown evident discomfort in the eyes, a trip to the vet is mandatory to ensure that other internal diseases are ruled out.

Symptoms of different eye problems in ducks

Avian Conjunctivitis

The most common symptoms of avian conjunctivitis include:

- Swollen eyelids
- Photosensitivity (the duck begins to avoid sunlight)

Avian conjunctivitis is the result of bacterial infection and is usually a sign of possible respiratory problems in the duck.

Uvelitis

The most common symptoms of uvelitis include:

- Inflammation in the inner regions of the eye
- Redness

Uvelitis is usually the precursor of cataract and must be treated immediately to avoid permanent blindness in the eye. It is almost always a sign of some other internal diseases in the bird.

Cataracts

The symptoms of cataract are similar to human beings. This includes:

- Formation of a translucent layer on the cornea

Cataract is the result of vitamin deficiency and may also be caused by continuous exposure to artificial lights. Other infections like uvelitis may also lead to cataracts in ducks. This makes them photosensitive and may also lead to permanent blindness in severe cases.

Marek's Disease

Common symptoms of Marek's Disease include:

- Irregular shape of the pupils
- Irritation in the eyes
- Iris disorders

- Blindness

Marek's disease may progress into cancer in worst cases. This is a viral infection that can be prevented with the suitable vaccination.

Avian Pox

Common symptoms of avian pox include:

- Swelling of the eyelids
- Formation of blisters
- Partial or total blindness

This is a viral infection that does not affect the eyeball. Therefore with the right kind of treatment, vision may be restored as well.

Causes of eye problems

There are several reasons why ducks contract eye problems. Some common factors leading to eye diseases in birds are:

- Bacterial infection, especially salmonella.
- Fungal infections due to moldy food and bedding
- Vitamin E deficiency

Treatment

Whenever you notice any redness, discharge or swelling in the eyes of your runner ducks, it is a sign of eye problems. Sometimes, the duck may blink too often, showing evident discomfort. To treat eye problems, you need to ensure that you attend to them in the earlier stages. Antibiotic eye drops and medicines are usually advised.

Other Common Diseases in Ducks

Botulism

Symptoms

- Limber neck with reduced muscular control
- Loss of Muscular control in limbs and wings
- Difficulty in swallowing properly

Causes

- Infection due to toxins produced by Clostridia bacterium

Treatment

- Ducks should be kept away from stagnant pools and dirty areas
- Provide fresh drinking water
- Epsom Salt may be added to the drinking water of the ducks

Coccidiosis

Symptoms

- Blood in the droppings
- Weight loss
- Persistent illness

Causes

- Contact with droppings of birds containing coccicdia. Droppings contain protozoa, making it difficult to eliminate them with just antibiotics.

Treatment

- Adding anticoccidial medication to the drinking water
- Keep the ground clean
- Feed them regularly

Duck Virus Enteritis

Entritis is very rare in ducks. However, if a bird is affected then it is highly likely that it will be fatal. The infection may be viral or bacterial. This condition is usually contagious and is acquired when domestic runner ducks come in contact with wild birds.

Symptoms

- Listlessness in birds
- Reddish or pinkish droppings

Treatment

- Antibiotic powders that dissolve in water. You must only give medicated water to the infected birds.

Duck Hepatitis

Hepatitis is most often contracted by ducklings and is fatal once the bird has been infected. This condition normally occurs when the duck is less than six weeks old.

Symptoms

- Severe spasticity
- Displacement of eyeballs within the orbit
- Paralysis
- Sudden death

Causes

- Hepatitis is caused due to two viruses in ducks. Duck Hepatitis Virus-1 and Duck Hepatitis Virus-2. Infection by DHV-1 is more severe, leading to the death of the duck within around two hours of the appearance of clinical symptoms

Treatment

Duck Hepatitis can only be prevented with vaccination.

Lead Poisoning

Symptoms

- Lack of coordination in the body
- Sudden loss of weight

Causes

- Lead shot form air gun pellets or cartridges

Treatment

- Remove the source of lead
- Give the ducks ample amount of grit.

Parasitic Infections

De-worming is an absolute must for ducks. They must be de-wormed twice a year, failing which, they will develop parasitic infections. There are several types of parasites that will affect Indian Runner Ducks.

- Gizzard Worms that affect the stomach
- Gapeworm that is usually found in the windpipe
- Caecal worms that are found in the gut
- Tapewoms
- Flukes

These parasites are usually carried by earthworms and insects that runner ducks consume when they are foraging. The only way to prevent this type of infection is providing the ducks with a clean environment where the presence of parasites is reduced.

Symptoms

- Continuous coughing
- Weight Loss
- Reduced Activity
- Dull Feathers
- Reduced Appetite

Treatment

Prescribed vermifuges mixed with the feed makes for the perfect treatment for parasitic infections in birds.

Cholera

Symptoms

- Reduced Appetite
- Increased thirst
- Lack of limb coordination

Causes

- Bacterial Infection

Treatment

- Antibiotics
- Elimination of carriers like rats

Riemerellaanatipestifer Infection

This infection is fatal in ducks. It is also found in other breeds of poultry like turkeys and geese. This condition normally occurs when the ducklings are between 1-8 weeks old.

Symptoms

- Stunted Growth
- Coughing
- Anorexia
- Diarrhea
- Convulsions
- Localized infections in chronic cases

Cause

Infection by gram-negative bacteria that belongs to Flavobacteriacae family.

Treatment

- Antibiotics
- Vaccination

Broken Wings in Ducks

Indian Runner ducks are flightless birds. Nevertheless, their wings form and important part of their defense mechanism and also help them maintain the balance of their bodies when they are running or walking upright. So, a broken wing is a serious issue that must be taken care of immediately.

You will require the assistance of a waterfowl vet to help take care of the issue completely. However, immediate first aid is necessary when you have a duck with a broken wing to ensure that the condition does not become worse.

There are several reasons why a duck might have a broken wing. If the drakes become aggressive, they are capable of getting injured in fights. Mating among ducks is so aggressive that, many times, the female might be attacked by several males at one time and actually breaks her wings. In addition to this, an attack by a predator may also cause serious injuries to ducks. There are always chances of the wing getting stuck in wires or mesh, leading to injuries like broken bones. Whatever the cause, broken wings can be very painful and must be take care of at the earliest.

How do you know if the wing is broken?

With flightless birds like the Indian runner duck, it is harder to notice a broken wing. You don't expect them to use their wings to fly around and, needless to say, you will probably notice a broken foot faster than the broken wing in these birds. However, a broken wing can cause excruciating pain and can lead to a lot of stress if left unattended. Sometimes, broken wings may also be accompanied by serious cuts and wounds that need to be treated properly to avoid infections. When a wing is broken, it will hang very low. You will notice that it is displaced and is much lower than the other wing.

How to calm the duck down

The first step is to gain the confidence of the bird to be able to handle it. Usually when they are injured, birds tend to become more defensive. Especially after an attack, a duck will not really be very easy to hold and take into your care. First, give the duck some feed and also some water. If he actually begins to eat, it is much easier for you to safely hold him. However, after a traumatizing injury, your duck is less likely to want to eat. In such cases, the only option you have is to coerce your duck into the nearest corner in order to catch him. You must be firm in your grip and gently hold the wings down, taking great care with the broken wing. The best way to calm a duck down is to set them in an isolated spot or even a small cage which is well lit and warm.

Healing a broken bone

You must approach an injured duck only when you are certain that it has calmed down completely. Failing this, you will find yourself going through the entire process of calming it down again.

Gently examine the bird for wounds and cuts that might be bleeding. These wounds must be washed to remove any impurity that might lead to infection. The wound can be washed with some lukewarm water or even iodine solution. If you have an antiseptic that you have used before, you may apply it.

The next step is to provide a splint or support of the broken wing. You can use sticky gauze or even veterinary tape for this purpose. Hold the wing in the natural position first. It must be held against the body of the bird to make sure that it heals in its natural position. Once the wing is in place, it needs to be bound to the body securely. Take the gauze or the tape around the body of the bird. The objective of the gauze and the tape is to ensure that the wing is immobilized. However, if you tie it too tightly, it might affect the breathing of the bird.

When you wrap the gauze, take it over the broken wing, around the body and under the wing that is functional. This will not restrict the movement of the other wing.

Usually, broken wings take about 4 weeks to heal completely. It is best that you keep the runner in a cage and in isolation until the wing is completely healed. During this period, if the gauze or tape becomes soiled, you may change it. If you notice that the duck is able to move the wing comfortably, you can remove the dressing. If not, you can take the gauze off after four weeks. Now your bird is also ready to mingle with the rest of the flock and carry on with his routine.

If your bird has been attacked by a predator, he might require vaccinations or shots to ensure that there is no infection. Even in case of open wounds, it is best recommended that you have it checked by a waterfowl professional.

Behavior Problems in Ducks

The most common behavior problems that occur in ducks are nipping, pinching and aggression. For most part, ducks are calm and compliant creatures. Behavior problems usually occur only when the ducks are 6 months of age or older. Aggression is a common problem with drakes who are ready to mate.

It is necessary to curb this type of behavior in the initial years to ensure that it does not persist. If your duck shows any aggressive behavior, a stern and sharp, 'NO' should do the trick. Ducks take time to view their owners as trustworthy companions and not predators.

Stress is also a problem with runner ducks. If you see your duck breathing with an open mouth, flapping his wings often and also refusing to interact with other ducks, then he is stressed. This may occur due to sudden change in location, extreme weather conditions or health issues.

Preventive Health care in Indian Runner Ducks

The first step towards rearing healthy ducks is preventing possible diseases and ailments. You can prevent several common diseases by maintaining the environment and the nutritional requirements of your Indian runner ducks.

- Keep your duck away from wild birds and animals. Using a fence is the most reliable option
- Vaccinations must be given on a regular basis to prevent diseases like hepatitis
- Routine checkups are mandatory.
- The coop of the ducks must be cleaned and disinfected on a regular basis.
- The foraging environment must be kept clean and hygienic
- The drinking water must be maintained and replaced every single day.
- Make sure you check the expiration date on the pellets that you feed them
- The bedding must be clean and dry
- The pens must be well ventilated

- Keep an eye on your bird to check for symptoms of illnesses.

Routine Check Up

Indian runner ducks must be taken to a waterfowl vet on a regular basis. Checking their feet, their wings, their beak and also their reproductive organs is a part of the routine checkup.

Finding a Waterfowl Vet

Waterfowl like the Indian runner ducks have special needs. They can only be treated by a certified avian veterinarian or a waterfowl veterinarian. When you are looking for a specialist who can take care of you Indian runners, make sure that he or she has ample experience with waterfowl as well as indoor birds. You can look for recommendations from people who already own pet ducks. You may also look online to locate a waterfowl vet close to your area.

Emergency and First Aid

If you notice injuries or sudden health problems in your Indian runner, choking for instance, you must be able to provide them with first aid. A well-equipped first aid kit is the first step towards ensuring immediate help for your birds. The must haves in your First Aid Kit are:

- **Tweezers:** Broken blood feathers are a common problem in runner ducks. If these feathers break or get damaged, they will bleed profusely. So it is recommended that you pluck them out gently using tweezers.

- **Blood Coagulant:** Injuries or breaking of blood feathers might cause profuse bleeding. Equipping yourself with some blood coagulant will help in case of an emergency.

- **Bag Balm:** This is a petroleum based products that can be used to soothe wounds and sores

- **Eye Ointment:** When ducks get into fights, they are most often prone to eye injuries. Having an antibacterial eye ointment can prevent severe infections.

- **Syringes or droppers:** In some conditions like sour crop, you might have to drop water or oil directly into the throat of the duck. Syringes and droppers can be used - also handy when you have to give your duck oral medication.

- **Rubber gloves:** Handling ducks with injuries puts you at the risk of infections. Using rubber gloves will keep you safe.

Chapter 5: Mating and Hatching

For those who plan to rear Indian Runner Ducks, it is important to understand how the ducklings need to be hatched and cared for. More importantly, understanding the changes that the ducks undergo during the mating season is essential.

Sexual Behavior in Indian Runner Ducks

One of the most surprising things about Indian Runner Ducks is the transformation in their behavior when they mate. Usually, ducks are very calm and even funny to watch. However, while mating their behavior is extremely aggressive. Of all the birds, ducks are considered to have the most violent sexual behavior.

Usually the females like to pick a suitable mating partner. Once she is convinced that she has found the right partner, she will show her consent by bobbing her head and by making loud and distinct quacks. Male ducks also court the females by putting their chest out and trotting majestically before them.

The only problem in a group of runner ducks is that one female will be attacked by more than one male. One possible explanation for this fact is that ducks are among the only three species of birds in the world that actually have a penis. This penis is long and can be twice the size of the duck's entire body. The penis will dry up and wither away once the mating season is over. As a result, ducks will be aggressive as they have the ability to mate only in one season.

Female ducks are quick to resist unwanted copulation. The most common behavior among female ducks is the voluntary closing of the vagina to avoid penetration. However, even if forceful insemination occurs, the vagina is designed in a way that stores the unwanted sperm and eliminates it after. So, female ducks have the final say in which duck will sire the next set of eggs.

The drakes will not usually stick around to help the hens raise the ducklings. They might be present only until the eggs hatch. However, there are instances when seasonal bonds are repeated with the same partner in the successive year - this means that the drake will come back to the same partner in the next mating season. This is a rare occurrence and is called philoparty.

Sex change in Ducks

It has been observed quite often by duck owners that their female duck undergoes a gender change. You will observe the occurrence of a tail curl in the ducks and also the appearance of drake coloring. Most often, when sex change occurs, the ducks will also stop laying eggs, however the primary sexual organs are never developed.

Several animal behavior specialists relate this drastic change to the forceful and aggressive sex that drakes engage in. Other scientists and waterfowl experts believe that the change occurs due to hormonal imbalances.

Breeding Ducks

Duck breeding is a very popular business model across the globe. Breeders choose to raise ducks for several reasons. With Indian runner ducks, the main reasons for breeding them is usually for a promising and lucrative egg business or the production of magnificent show birds for exhibitors.

Why Choose Duck Breeding

After chickens, ducks are the most sought after birds for breeding. Today, with the convenience of scientific breeding, there are several advantages of breeding ducks since the scope is higher. Some of the advantages of choosing to breed ducks over other poultry include:

- **Easy to handle:** Ducks are not as demanding as other poultry. They are happy with their own flocks and are not too attention seeking or even sensitive as other birds.

- **Easy to maintain**: In comparison to other poultry and farm fowl, runner ducks are tougher. They do not get infected by several parasites and are also immune to several avian diseases. So, healthcare is not as expensive and feeding is also not an issue with these ducks.

- **Not Demanding**: Ducks can thrive in several kinds of environments. They can be bred even on riversides and wetlands. They are also ideal for integrated farming because of their pleasant nature

- **Egg Laying**: Runner Ducks are known for their prolific egg laying. In a given season, these birds lay over 150 eggs.

- Ducks are pleasant and will seldom display aggressive behavior.

- After the eggs have hatched, runner ducklings are the easiest to sex. Therefore they are very simple to handle and maintain.

Natural or Selective Breeding?

Natural breeding is where the ducks are allowed to mate with their own kind to produce offspring. Over several decades, features and characteristics that threaten the survival of a species are modified or eliminated. According to Charles Darwin, only those breeds that are fittest to survive will carry the lineage forward. This process is called natural selection. Natural breeding is a great option for breeders who are only interested in having ducks for their eggs, meat or for ornamental purposes.

Artificial breeding is the process of using only those birds with desirable characteristics for mating. This procedure is ideal for people who are into breeding for showing and exhibition. There are several interesting breeds that are the result of mating Peking ducks with Runner Ducks. The color mutations in the plumage of the Indian runner ducks are a perfect example of selective breeding. The only drawback of selective breeding is the possibility of severe mutations that lead to offspring that are poorly developed or even too weak to survive, sometimes.

Questions to ask yourself before breeding ducks

Breeding Indian runner ducks is not an easy task. You must be prepared to invest a lot of time and energy to transform this into a lucrative business, there are several questions that you must ask yourself.

- What is the purpose of breeding the ducks?
- Do I have ample space to provide the ducks with an environment that will allow them to thrive healthily?
- Do I have the funds to invest in the ducks and their care?
- Do I have ample help to deal with the demands of duck breeding?
- Will I be able to keep the ducks away from obvious dangers like predators?
- Are my neighbors ok with it?
- What are the licenses that I need to keep ducks and breed them legally?
- Does my breeding program require any certification?

Hatching and Incubation

Indian Runner Ducks will start laying eggs when they are about 7 months old. Each duck will lay about 150-200 hundred eggs each year. It is a challenge to collect these eggs and hatch them successfully. There are two ways of hatching the eggs:

- Natural Incubation
- Artificial incubation

Natural Incubation

When a female actually sits on the eggs to hatch them, the process is known as brooding. A hen that is ready for brooding will show obvious signs. She will stop laying eggs and will make a very evident quacking noise, often refusing to budge.

In order to increase hatchability of the eggs, you must ensure that there are not more than 15 eggs on each nest. Once the hen begins to brood, she will provide the eggs with the right amount of moisture and heat required for the eggs to hatch.

When you have a broody egg you must take care of the following:

- Feed and water should be kept close
- The feed must be modified to suit the nutritional requirements of the brooding ducks.
- The ducks must be checked regularly for parasites and also for infections

After the first week of brooding, you must check these eggs for fertility. Simply hold them up against any bright light. If there is an evident dark shape in the egg, you can be certain that it is fertile. If it is clear, the egg is infertile.

Artificial Incubation

If the eggs are collected regularly, runner ducks will not become broody. In such cases, artificial incubation is the only option. Commercial incubators are available to help you hatch the eggs. These incubators vary in capacity and most often depend upon electricity, gas or kerosene to provide heat. The temperature of the device may be regulated using a thermostat that comes along with the incubator. The Indian runner duck will take about 28 days to hatch when kept in an incubator.

Once the eggs are removed from storage, they must be kept in room temperature for at least 6 hours before they are transferred in to the incubator. The temperature must be set to 37.5 degree Celsius and must be reduced by 0.2 degrees in case of hatchers.

Humidity must also be just right. If it is excessive, the eggs won't dry sufficiently to hatch. If it is less, the drying occurs too quickly. You can use moisture trays to control humidity, ideally be set at 70% relative humidity.

The eggs in the incubator must be turned every day to make sure that the contents do not stick to the shell. Usually, the eggs are turned at an angle of 90 degrees. This process can be automated using turning equipment that will turn the eggs every hour.

You can check the eggs for fertilization by shining a bright light on them. One important process in artificial incubation is fumigation. A mixture of formalin and potassium permanganate may be used to get rid of harmful bacteria, especially salmonella.

Removing the Hatch from the Incubator

Once the eggs are close to the hatching date, you must prepare a brooder with the required heat source. Hatchability in ducks is usually about 70%. The hatch must be transferred to the brooder almost as soon as it the process is complete.

Brooders are necessary even when you opt for natural incubation. When the eggs are about to hatch, you will see that the hen sits on them for shorter periods of time.

Once the ducklings have hatched, they should be given growers pellets as feed. These pellets contain the necessary nutrients and minerals for the ducklings to develop properly. Once the ducklings are about five weeks old, wheat can be introduced with grit. Grit usually consists of oyster shells and helps provide the roughage necessary to break the food down while digesting.

Can you Avoid Artificial Incubation?

Although there are no recorded issues with artificial incubation, there are some breeders who prefer natural incubation. If you have noticed that your runner ducks have stopped brooding, you can reintroduce them to this concept using model eggs and even rocks. There are some breeds of chicken that can be replaced to incubate the eggs naturally as well. When you pick another breeder for your duck eggs, make sure you check the brooding and mothering history of the bird.

Reproductive Problems in Birds

Egg Binding

Egg binding is a common oviduct problem that prevents the duck from laying eggs. The egg descends into the lower oviduct and is held up there. This condition is quite common in younger females who have just started laying. This problem may also occur in case of severe cold weather during the breeding season.

Symptoms

A duck that is about to lay eggs will:

- Spend most of her time on cage floor
- They will strain by bobbing their tail up and down to pass the egg
- Breathing problems
- Constipation
- Fluffed Feathers

Treatment

- Provide mixed poultry grit
- Calcium, Phosphorous and vitamin D supplements can be given
- Keep the duck in warm areas

Oviduct Prolapse

Sometimes, the oviduct protrudes in the lower region. This condition usually occurs when the duck has difficulty in passing the egg out.

Treatment

- Provide calcium and phosphorous supplements
- Feed should only include layers pellets
- Keep the duck warm
- Oral medication or injections if the problem persists.

Exposed Penis

Usually, in runner ducks the penis cannot be retracted causing it to drop externally from the body. This may head to infections if it persists. Waterfowl experts associate the upright position of the bird with this problem.

Treatment

- Keep the environment sanitary and clean
- Provide the bird with lots of drinking water

Meritis

Bacterial infection of the oviduct, leading to inflammation is known as meritis.

Symptoms

- Persistent vaginal discharge
- Loss of appetite
- Lethargy

Treatment

- Antibodies administered orally or through injections

Peritonitis

Peritonitis is usually the result of an ovarian prolapse. When the egg fails to make its way into the oviduct but goes into the abdominal cavity instead, peritonitis occurs. The lining of the abdomen called the peritoneum gets infected.

Symptoms

- Swelling around the abdomen
- Diarrhea
- Sudden Death

Treatment

- Antibiotics have been effective in some cases.

Will your Duck Stop Laying Eggs?

Although runner ducks are known for their amazing egg laying abilities, there are some occasions when they simply will not produce any eggs. Most often, this is a sign of a reproductive. However, there are several other factors that might have lead to a stop in egg laying:

- **The age of the bird**: The number of eggs laid will reduce as the duck ages and may eventually come to a halt.

- **Parasites**: If your duck is suffering from any problem related to parasites and ticks, she might be unable to produce healthy eggs. In some cases, the entire process of egg formation is hindered, leading to a stop in the laying of eggs.

- **Weather conditions**: Ducks are able to produce eggs only when they have ample warmth. In case the weather is not suitable for your duck to produce eggs you can expect her to be unable to do so.

- **Change in Diet:** If you are contemplating a change in your duck's diet, it must be done gradually. You must also make sure that the duck has enough time until the breeding season to get used to a certain kind of diet. If the nutrition is not adequate or is different from what your duck is used to, there is a hindrance in the production of the egg.

- **New Birds in the Flock:** When ducks interact in a group, they tend to be extremely social and also form a pecking order. When you introduce one or more new ducks, this equation changes. The ducks become stressed a nd will stop laying eggs for some time until the pecking order has been re-established.

- **Change in Routine:** Ducks are highly disciplined creatures. They need to be fed at a certain time and must also be allowed to roost at a certain time. However, if you make any significant change in any part of their routine, it leads to severe stress, thus halting the egg laying process.

- **Improper Husbandry:** If the pen is unclean or overcrowded, the number of eggs laid will reduce significantly. In addition, if the conditions of the pen are too dark or cold, it results in stress and illness

How to Increase Egg Laying

There are several steps you can take as the breeder and the owner of your flock to make sure that the egg production is consistent. These simple measures are also very important in ensuring that your eggs are healthy and of great quality.

- **Check the quality of the feed:** When you purchase the feed from pet stores or the supermarket, you will see that there are several options available. You must make sure that you make no compromises on costs and other factors and only choose recommended duck feed pellets. Make sure that the feed is fresh, has no insects and mold in it and is also compliant with the recommended nutrient levels.

- **Correct quantity and type of feed:** The type of food that you choose for your duck must be appropriate for its age. For instance, if you have chicks, make sure you feed them grower pellets instead of regular pellets. On an average, a duck that is ready to lay eggs must be put on a controlled diet. She should be given not more than .35 pounds per day - an overweight duck will develop issues with fertility and egg production.

- **Good Quality of Water:** If you are unable to ensure that the water is clean, you will see that egg production is hindered. Water is required in order for ducks to regulate their body temperature – this is pivotal in the process of laying eggs. If the water is muddy or messy, your ducks will become stressed and depressed to an extent.

- **Ensure proper lighting:** Day length is an important concept for ducks that are breeding. Usually, a duck becomes sexually mature only when the length of the day begins to increase. This is between the months of January and June. When the day length begins to reduce, egg production also comes to a halt. If you want your ducks to continue laying eggs, you must make up for the lack of natural light with artificial light. Your runner duck must have at least 17 hours of sunlight every day. This, of course, is greater than the natural light available. In order for your duck to get comfortable with this, make sure you add ½ hour of light each day before sunrise and after sunset each week till you reach 17 hours of light.

- **Do not have too many males in the group:** Usually, the recommended ration of females to males is 1:5. If you add more males to the group, they could become violent.

Conservation of rare species

Farmers, scientists and enthusiastic breeders are constantly devising new methods to preserve rear breeds of birds and animals. The Indian Runner duck is recognized as a pure breed wonder because of its unusual posture and body shape. Of course several color mutations are available due to experimentation and development of the breed. The runners are preserved by organizations like the Livestock Conservancy that is dedicated to maintaining purebred farm animals and birds.

They have a large gene bank consisting of genetic strains form purebred animals. This gene bank allows them to maintain healthy populations of rare species to ensure that they do not become endangered. These organizations also establish standards to define the purebred species of poultry and farm animals.

Guidelines for Showing

Indian runner ducks make great birds for showing and exhibiting. There are certain guidelines to determine whether a certain duck is suitable for showing or not. These guidelines have been set by the British Waterfowl Association. To qualify, a duck should have:

- An upright carriage
- A lean and racy head with a wedge shaped bill
- Long and slender neck that is in line with the body
- Centrally placed eyes
- Long, narrow and cylindrical body
- Downward extended tail when the bird is alert
- Legs that are set far apart
- Tight and smooth plumage
- Weight: Drake 1.6–2.3 kg (3 ½ – 5 lb)
  Duck 1.4–2.0 kg (3 – 4 ½ lb)

Usually the birds are scored out of 100. The distribution of the points are as follows:

- Carriage: 20 points
- Neck, head and bill: 20 points
- Body: 20 points
- Legs and feet: 5 points
- Color: 15 points
- Condition : 10 points
- Size 10 points

If the duck has obvious deformities such as a deformed bill, poor carriage, dome shaped head and prominent shoulders, it leads to disqualification.

Chapter 6: Runner Duck Eggs

Duck eggs are gaining popularity over chicken eggs across the globe for their nutritional value

Characteristics of Runner Duck Eggs:

Here are some basic characteristics of runner duck eggs:

Color:	**White, off white, blue and light green**
Size:	**Same as a large hen's egg**
Weight:	**60-70 grams**

Nutritional Value:

- 9.5 gms of protein per egg
- 108-130 calories
- 619 mg cholesterol
- 7.3 gms of fat
- Vitamins B6, B12, A, D, E
- 8 essential amino acids
- Phosphorous and Calcium
- Sulphur
- Zinc
- Potassium
- Iron

Although duck eggs have high cholesterol content, the egg yolk contains choline which is effective in reducing harmful effects of cholesterol. In fact, studies indicate that people who consume duck eggs are less likely to have higher levels of bad cholesterol.

Routine and Collection

On average Runner ducks lay up to 150 eggs per year. They often do not restrict the egg-laying to a nest. So, keep alert and try to collect the eggs as and when they are laid, this prevents breakage and wastage.

Collecting Eggs

Usually ducks tend to lay eggs early in the morning or late at night. When you are collecting eggs and your duck is still laying eggs, it is best that you allow the duck to roost for at least two hours before you proceed to select the next batch of eggs. Eggs must always be collected in the plastic egg trays. It is advisable to keep the dirty and clean eggs separate.

If you are selecting eggs for incubation, you must make sure that the egg is not underweight, cracked or molted and poor in texture. These eggs are less likely to hatch and are better for human consumption.

Cleaning

Eggs must be cleaned as soon as they have been collected to ensure that they do not get spoiled. There are several microorganisms that might make their way in to the shell if the eggs are not cleaned. To remove the mud and manure, the eggs can be rubbed gently with steel wool. Wiping them after this is also an option.

Storage

If you do not have enough eggs to incubate, you may have to store the ones that you already have. These eggs can be stored for a maximum of seven days before they are incubated. It is best to store them in cold conditions. Maintain the temperature at about 13 degrees Celsius, with 75% relative humidity. Always keep the pointed end of the egg down for maximum hatchability.

Chapter 8: Duck Egg Recipes

Duck eggs are high in protein, iron, calcium, potassium and other minerals and are therefore a much healthier choice than chicken eggs.

Since they taste similar to chicken eggs and are almost the same size, it is pretty easy to incorporate duck eggs into your recipes.

The national organization, Local Harvest, which helps people in finding fresh and organic food, has stated that duck eggs are a healthier option as it contains almost 6 times vitamin D and twice the quantity of vitamin A, as compared to chicken eggs. Ducks eggs are also richer in Omega-3 fatty acids, Vitamin E and B.

On the contrary, duck eggs have one drawback; the cholesterol content in duck eggs is higher as compared to chicken eggs. However the high levels of Vitamin B act to reduce cholesterol absorption in the body.

- **Duck eggs have a thicker shell and hence stay fresh for a longer period**
- **They are much superior nutritionally and hence a healthy choice**
- **They are rich and dense and contain extra albumen which helps in making pastries and cakes fluffy and rich.**
- **They are a rich source of Omega 3 fatty acids that is extremely essential for the body, be it for brain health or skin care.**
- **Duck eggs are one of the few foods that promote alkaline production in the body. Alkaline is important for cancer patients as an alkaline environment doesn't allow cancer cells to thrive. On the other hand chicken eggs produce more acids in the body.**

Shelf Life of Duck Eggs as Opposed to Chicken Eggs

Ducks eggs have a tougher shell, which is much difficult to crack as compared to a chicken egg shell. This thick shell is responsible for a longer shelf life. When we say longer shelf life, a duck egg can stay fresh for almost 6 weeks without losing its nutrition if it is well refrigerated.

The yolk to egg white ratio is also higher in a duck egg, so when you need more yolk for cooking or baking purpose, it makes more sense to opt for a duck egg.

Nutrition Quotient of Duck Eggs as Opposed to Chicken Eggs

- The yolk of a duck egg is much darker in color than a chicken egg, which denotes denser nutrition.

- Duck eggs contain 6 x the Vitamin D, 2 x the Vitamin A and about 75% of Vitamin E that is available in chicken eggs.

- Duck eggs also have a higher Vitamin K2 content and are higher in calories, possibly due to its extra fat content, so an ideal meal for those who need a high calorie diet. Typically, a 100 gm duck egg contains about 185 kcal of energy as opposed to 149 kcal of energy available in a chicken egg.

- Both chicken and duck eggs are have equal carbohydrate content; although, duck eggs are higher in protein content.

- Both eggs contain selenium, zinc, manganese, copper, sodium, potassium, calcium, phosphorus and iron.

- Duck eggs have a higher amount of thiamine, riboflavin, niacin, folate, pantothenic acids, B6 and B12 and retinol.

- The amino acid content of duck eggs is higher than chicken eggs. The amino acids include threonine, methionine, isoleucine, cystine, tryptophan, valine, leucine, lysine, tyrosine, phenylalanine, serine, proline, aspartic acid, glycine histidine, arginine, and alanine.

We all know several ways of cooking with chicken eggs. If you have just switched to duck eggs, here are my five favorite recipes.

Smoked Salmon with Asparagus and Special Duck Egg Scramble

Ingredients

Duck Eggs	3
Butter	1 stick
Sour Cream	1 tsp
Smoked Salmon	200 gms
Bread	1 slice
Asparagus	6 spears
Chives	For garnishing
Salt and Pepper	To taste

Instructions

- Steam the asparagus for about 4 minutes.
- Break the duck eggs in a large saucepan.
- Add butter and work the eggs with a spatula. You may want to keep the heat low to avoid burning.
- Make sure your bread has been set to toast just before the eggs are ready.
- The eggs should be cooked between 4-5 mins according to taste
- Pour sour cream over the eggs and add salt and pepper.
- Chop the salmon and fold it into the mixture of eggs and sour cream.
- Serve with asparagus, toast and a sprinkling of chives.

Toasted Duck Egg Sandwich

Ingredients

- Butter   1 stick
- Duck eggs   1 for each set
- Bread   2 slices per set
- Salt and pepper   To taste

Instructions

- Break your duck eggs into a small bowl and beat gently.
- Add the seasoning.
- Butter the slices of bread.
- Place the bottom slice in the toaster with the buttered side down.
- Pour over beaten eggs and cover with the other slice, buttered side up.
- Toast until the edges are brown.
- The sandwich will have a runny centre which adds to the devouring experience.

Duck Egg & Cheese Omelet

Ingredients

- Duck eggs   2
- Hard Cheese   50 gms
- Olive Oil   1 tablespoon
- Salt and pepper   To taste
- Salad Cress   For garnishing

Instructions

- Break the ducks eggs in a small bowl and beat with seasoning.
- Heat the olive oil in a pan and pour in beaten eggs.
- When the eggs are almost cooked add grated cheese and allow to melt.

- Just before you toss the egg, add the salad cress.
- Serve with a side of asparagus and toast.

Coddled Egg with Bruschetta and Fresh Herbs

Ingredients

• Duck Egg	1
• Butter	1 stick
• Bread Stick Slices	3
• Garlic	1 clove
• Olive oil	1 teaspoon
• Salt and pepper	To taste

Instructions

- Take a small porcelain dish and place it in a pot with boiling water.
- Break the egg into a bowl and add seasoning. Beat gently.
- Grease the insides of the coddler/ porcelain dish with butter.
- Pour the egg into the porcelain dish/coddler and cover it tightly.
- Ideally, the water must come up to at least 2/3rds the height of the side of your coddler.
- Allow the egg to cook slowly till the middle is runny (4 minutes)
- If you take the egg out and find that it is not fully done, all you need to do is put it back in the coddler and turn the heat on.
- Toast the slices of bread till they are golden brown on either side.
- Peel and crush the garlic clove and rub it gently on one side of the toast.
- Drizzle with olive oil
- Garnish with some chopped herbs and serve with the coddled eggs.

Index

Index

Index

Printed in Great Britain
by Amazon